VOLUME I

Perspectives on Technical Information for Environmental Protection

A report to the
U.S. Environmental Protection Agency
from the
Commission on Natural Resources
and the
Steering Committee for Analytical Studies

National Research Council

NATIONAL ACADEMY OF SCIENCES
Washington, D.C. 1977

This study was supported by the Environmental Protection Agency.
Contract No. 68-01-2430

Library of Congress Catalog Card Number 77-80535
International Standard Book Number 0-309-02623-7

Available from

Printing and Publishing Office
National Academy of Sciences
2101 Constitution Avenue
Washington, D.C. 20418

Printed in the United States of America

March 18, 1977

The Honorable Douglas M. Costle
Administrator
Environmental Protection Agency
Washington, D.C.

Dear Mr. Costle:

I am pleased to transmit a report entitled "Perspectives on Technical Information for Environmental Protection," the first of a series prepared under Contract No. 68-01-2430 as provided in P.L. 93-135. This report distills the principal conclusions garnered by the National Research Council, led by our Commission on Natural Resources, as we attempted to meet the concerns expressed by the House Appropriations Subcommittee on Agriculture, Environment and Consumer Protection (now the Subcommittee on HUD and Independent Agencies) in House Report 93-275, dated 12 June 1973.

Ten major studies were mounted in all, engaging the efforts of some 200 scientists, engineers, physicians, and attorneys. This report includes executive summaries of those four studies with major implications for the formulation of environmental policy. This and the ten reports to follow, collectively, constitute our response to the charge offered by the House Subcommittee.

The Perspectives here presented are not merely a summary of the reports to follow. They offer both a philosophy and specific recommendations to help guide both the Environmental Protection Agency and the nation as we seek to protect our people and preserve and enhance our national heritage. Subsequent reports will concern themselves, in some part, with previous decisions and regulations. However, the present Perspectives and the individual reports are addressed to the future and the multiple facets of what is required to assure that wisdom and our full national scientific capabilities are brought to bear in the management of the Agency's great responsibilities.

The more technical reports to follow will each be of interest to a somewhat specialized audience. These Perspectives are commended to the attention of all citizens who share our concern for the quality of our environment.

Sincerely yours,

PHILIP HANDLER, *President*
National Academy of Sciences

v

COMMISSION ON NATURAL RESOURCES

*GORDON J.F. MACDONALD *(Chairman)*, Dartmouth College

*WILLIAM C. ACKERMANN, Illinois State Water Survey
THOMAS D. BARROW , Exxon Corporation
*JOHN E. CANTLON, Michigan State University
DAYTON H. CLEWELL, Mobil Oil Corporation, retired
HAROLD L. JAMES, U.S. Geological Survey
JULIUS E. JOHNSON, Dow Chemical U.S.A.
ALLEN V. KNEESE, University of New Mexico
C.C. MCCORKLE, JR., University of California
H. WILLIAM MENARD, Scripps Institute of Oceanography
NORMAN A. PHILLIPS, National Oceanic and Atmospheric Administration
WILLIAM K. REILLY, The Conservation Foundation
*ROBERT M. SOLOW, Massachusetts Institute of Technology
E. BRIGHT WILSON, Harvard University

Ex Officio Members

NORMAN HACKERMAN, Rice University *(Chairman,* Board on Energy Studies)
ELBURT F. OSBORN, Carnegie Institution of Washington *(Chairman,* Board on Mineral Resources)
GILBERT F. WHITE, University of Colorado *(Chairman,* Environmental Studies Board)
SYLVAN WITTWER, Michigan State University *(Chairman,* Board on Agriculture and Renewable Resources)

RICHARD A. CARPENTER, *Executive Director*

*Also members of the Steering Committee for Analytical Studies

vi

ENVIRONMENTAL STUDIES BOARD

Contents

Foreword

This report is one of a series prepared by the National Research Council for the U.S. Environmental Protection Agency.

In June 1973 the Subcommittee on Agriculture, Environmental, and Consumer Protection of the Appropriations Committee of the U.S. House of Representatives held extensive hearings on the activities of EPA, and the ensuing appropriations bill for fiscal year 1974 directed the Agency to contract with the National Academy of Sciences for a series of analytical advisory studies (87 Stat. 482, PL 93-135). EPA and the Academy agreed upon a program that would respond to the Congressional intent by exploring two major areas: the process of acquisition and use of scientific and technical information in environmental regulatory decision making; and the analysis of selected current environmental problems. The Academy directed the National Research Council to formulate an approach to the analytical studies, and the National Research Council in turn designated the Commission on Natural Resources as the unit responsible for supervising the program.

The other studies in the series, and a diagram of the structure of the program are presented on the following pages. Each of the component studies has issued a report on its findings. This volume, *Perspectives on Technical Information for Environmental Protection,* is the report of the Steering Committee for Analytical Studies and the Commission on Natural Resources. It describes in detail the origins of the program and summarizes and comments on the more detailed findings and judgments in the other reports.

Components of the NRC Program of Analytical Studies for the
U.S. Environmental Protection Agency

Project	Project Chairman	Sponsoring Unit of the NRC
Steering Committee for Analytical Studies (SCAS)	R. M. Solow	Commission on Natural Resources
Environmental Decision Making (CEDM)	J. P. Ruina	Environmental Studies Board, Committee on Public Engineering Policy
Environmental Research Assessment (ERAC)	J. M. Neuhold	Environmental Studies Board
Environmental Monitoring (SGEM)	J. W. Pratt	Committee on National Statistics, Environmental Studies Board, Numerical Data Advisory Board
Environmental Manpower (CSEM)	E. F. Gloyna	Commission on Human Resources
Energy and the Environment (CEE)	S. I. Auerbach	Board on Energy Studies
Pesticide Decision Making	W. G. Eden	Board on Agriculture and Renewable Resources, Environmental Studies Board
Multimedium Approach to Municipal Sludge Management	H. O. Banks	Environmental Studies Board
Societal Consequences of Transportation Noise Abatement	W. J. Baumol	Assembly of Behavioral and Social Sciences[b]
Disposal in the Marine Environment	D. S. Gorsline	Ocean Affairs Board
Review of Management of EPA's Research Activities	R. W. Berliner	Commission on Natural Resources

[a]In cooperation with the Building Research Advisory Board.
[b]In cooperation with the Building Research Advisory Board and the Transportation Research Board.

Structure of the NRC Program of Analytical Studies for the U.S. Environmental Protection Agency

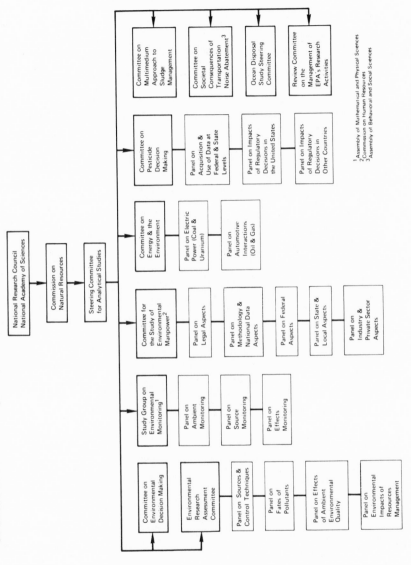

National Research Council
National Academy of Sciences

Commission on Natural Resources

Steering Committee for Analytical Studies

Committee on Environmental Decision Making
- Environmental Research Assessment Committee
- Panel on Sources & Control Techniques
- Panel on Fates of Pollutants
- Panel on Effects of Ambient Environmental Quality
- Panel on Environmental Impacts of Resources Management

Study Group on Environmental Monitoring[1]
- Panel on Ambient Monitoring
- Panel on Source Monitoring
- Panel on Effects Monitoring

Committee for the Study of Environmental Manpower[2]
- Panel on Legal Aspects
- Panel on Methodology & National Data Aspects
- Panel on Federal Aspects
- Panel on State & Local Aspects
- Panel on Industry & Private Sector Aspects

Committee on Energy & the Environment
- Panel on Electric Power (Coal & Uranium)
- Panel on Automotive Interactions (Oil & Gas)

Committee on Pesticide Decision Making
- Panel on Acquisition & Use of Data at Federal & State Levels
- Panel on Impacts of Regulatory Decisions in the United States
- Panel on Impacts of Regulatory Decisions in Other Countries

- Committee on Multimedium Approach to Sludge Management
- Committee on Societal Consequences of Transportation Noise Abatement[3]
- Ocean Disposal Study Steering Committee
- Review Committee on the Management of EPA's Research Activities

[1] Assembly of Mathematical and Physical Sciences
[2] Commission on Human Resources
[3] Assembly of Behavioral and Social Sciences

xiii

I PERSPECTIVES ON TECHNICAL INFORMATION FOR ENVIRONMENTAL PROTECTION

1 Introduction

PURPOSE OF THE REPORT

Perspectives on Technical Information for Environmental Protection is intended as a summary of and commentary on the more detailed and concrete findings and judgments embodied in the main reports of the series of National Research Council analytical studies for the U.S. Environmental Protection Agency. The report represents a broad consensus of those scientists and engineers who, as members of the Steering Committee for Analytical Studies and the Commission on Natural Resources, led the work of some 200 experts in studies of the acquisition and use of scientific information by the EPA. It is, of course, not to be expected that each member of the Steering Committee and the Commission will agree with every statement presented here.

The report should be read as an overview in the broader context of the series of individual analytical studies themselves, each of which presents the detailed documentation and more extended rationale essential to its specific recommendations. Those component studies (see Table 1) are the formal product of the program, and the interested reader should refer to them as the basis of the commentary made here.

The executive summaries of four of the reports that have principal implications for environmental regulatory policy are included in Part II of this volume; the complete reports have also been published separately. All the analytical studies were not available in final form as this volume went to press, but the work of the study committees had progressed

TABLE 1   Components of the NRC Program of Analytical Studies for the U.S. Environmental Protection Agency

Project	Project Chairman	Sponsoring Unit of the NRC
Steering Committee for Analytical Studies (SCAS)	R. M. Solow	Commission on Natural Resources
Environmental Decision Making (CEDM)	J. P. Ruina	Environmental Studies Board, Committee on Public Engineering Policy
Environmental Research Assessment (ERAC)	J. M. Neuhold	Environmental Studies Board
Environmental Monitoring (SGEM)	J. W. Pratt	Committee on National Statistics, Environmental Studies Board, Numerical Data Advisory Board
Environmental Manpower (CSEM)	E. F. Gloyna	Commission on Human Resources
Energy and the Environment (CEE)	S. I. Auerbach	Board on Energy Studies
Pesticide Decision Making	W. G. Eden	Board on Agriculture and Renewable Resources, Environmental Studies Board[a]
Multimedium Approach to Municipal Sludge Management	H. O. Banks	Environmental Studies Board
Societal Consequences of Transportation Noise Abatement	W. J. Baumol	Assembly of Behavioral and Social Sciences[b]
Disposal in the Marine Environment	D. S. Gorsline	Ocean Affairs Board
Review of Management of EPA's Research Activities	R. W. Berliner	Commission on Natural Resources

[a]In cooperation with the Building Research Advisory Board.
[b]In cooperation with the Building Research Advisory Board and the Transportation Research Board.

sufficiently to allow these perspectives to be drawn from the program. This volume is being released now to assist the new Administration and the Congress at a time when the analyses and advisory recommendations of the NRC program could be most helpful.

In the course of work there were extensive discussions among EPA officials and the scientists, engineers, and other experts who served on the National Research Council committees. Suggestions for enhancement of the acquisition and use of scientific information evolved during these meetings and, in a number of instances, were rapidly implemented by the Agency. Thus, some of the recommendations in these reports will be perceived as reinforcing changes and trends in EPA operations that are already under way.

HISTORY OF THE ANALYTICAL STUDIES PROGRAM

The Environmental Protection Agency came into being on December 2, 1970. It had been proposed by Reorganization Plan No. 3 on July 9 of that year. The new independent agency was created to administer an amalgamation of pollution control programs established by separate laws over the previous decade. No new organic act was involved in its formation, and it was given no jurisdiction over federal programs to develop and allocate natural resources. Its mission is to protect the environment by preventing and abating pollution.

Jurisdiction over funding for the EPA was placed with the (then) House Appropriations Subcommittee on Agriculture, Environment, and Consumer Protection (now the Subcommittee on HUD and Independent Agencies). In House Report 93-275, June 12, 1973, the Subcommittee expressed concern that environmental protection regulations were being set in an unsystematic and inconsistent manner that did not properly consider their economic and social impacts. The Subcommittee suggested reasons for the deficiencies, as it perceived them, including the piecemeal approach mandated by the various pollution control laws and the inadequate use of scientific information and technical judgment in regulatory decision making. To quote from the Committee's report:

Because of all the problems discussed above, the Committee recommends an appropriation of $5,000,000 for a complete and thorough review of the programs of the Environmental Protection Agency. The studies shall be conducted under contract with the National Academy of Sciences which has a reputation for technical competence and complete objectivity, and shall include, but not be limited to:

(1) The estimated cost of pollution abatement activities over the next decade and the benefits to be derived versus the cost. (If we are to spend $287 billion over the next decade, as estimated by EPA, how can we get the maximum pollution control for our money?);

(2) The degree to which environmental regulations have contributed or will contribute to the current and the long-term energy crisis;

(3) The effect of emission control standards on the cost and performance of automobiles, including the cost/benefit implications of present standards;

(4) The benefits and hazards to humans of agricultural and home use chemicals, such as pesticides, herbicides, rodenticides and fertilizers; and the effect on food and fiber production and the protection of human health of the inability to use those chemicals now banned or restricted; and

(5) The utilization of scientific and technical personnel and the identification of policy level positions that should be staffed with scientific or technical personnel.

The Committee feels that this study will provide the information needed to better assess where we are headed and whether or not the cost of getting there is equal to the benefits. EPA will be expected to submit periodic reports to the Committee on the progress of these studies. Copies of the final report shall be provided to the appropriate executive departments and agencies and to the Congress.

The House and Senate Appropriations Committees were advised that under the terms of its charter to respond when called upon, the National Academy of Sciences (NAS) would make appropriate studies of the acquisition and use of scientific and technical information in environmental regulatory decision making, but that it would not undertake to audit or review the Agency's performance. This position was agreeable to Congress, and the item providing $5 million for the study remained in the appropriations bill when it passed into law (PL 93-135, approved October 24, 1973, 87 Stat. 482).

Subsequent negotiations with EPA developed a program of studies (see Figure 1) responsive to the language of the House report and practicable for the resources and methods of the NAS and its operating institution, the National Research Council. The Commission on Natural Resources was assigned management responsibility for the program. Decisions about the studies to be undertaken reflected mutual agreement based on relevance to the central theme of acquisition and use of scientific and technical knowledge, the concerns of Congress, and avoidance of retrospective judgment about the correctness of a regulation. Decisions pending or in litigation were to be avoided so that the studies would not affect or delay proceedings. The independence of the National Research Council was maintained in such matters as appointment of study committee members, development of the approach and methods to be followed, and determination of findings, conclusions, and recommendations. A performance period of three years was agreed upon from 28 June 1974 to 27 June 1977.

The program of studies is shown in Table 1. Four of the projects analyzed major functional components of environmental regulation: decision making, research, monitoring, and manpower. Six other projects dealt in greater detail with specific environmental problems: energy and the environment, transportation noise, pesticides, sludge from municipal sewage treatment plants, and ocean disposal. Each of these studies illustrated the role of technical information in decision making. (See Table 2 for the titles of these reports.) At an early stage in the program, the Administrator of EPA asked for an immediate review of research management in the Agency. A report on that review was issued in September 1974.[1]

Comparison of the program, as it has been carried out, with the language of the House report reflects the results of negotiations with the Agency and of planning within the National Research Council. The requests for study of the costs and benefits of pollution control were considered to have been substantially met by two ongoing projects: a study by the Academy for the Senate Public Works Committee of air pollution from the automobile and stationary sources (NRC 1974a, 1974b, 1974c, 1974d, 1975a); and a study for the National Commission on Water Quality calling for review of all aspects of water pollution control (NCWQ 1976). The applications of cost–benefit analysis were examined in these projects, and the ensuing reports were resource documents for the Committee on Environmental Decision Making.

A study on transportation noise and another on management of sludge from municipal sewage treatment plants were added to provide substantive analyses of critical environmental issues. The first of these was chosen to illustrate a relatively new area of pollution control in which procedures have not yet become routine. The second topic was chosen to highlight problems common to many pollution control questions in which the various disposal media cannot safely be treated in isolation. Along with the studies on energy, pesticides, and ocean disposal, these were to focus on specific problems of decision making and to serve as case studies for the more general analyses.

Not all the funds allocated were spent: the program was limited to a practical and useful effort to answer the questions posed by Congress and the Agency.

The methods used by the study committees in gathering information for their deliberations were appropriate to the task, which was an independent analysis of the means by which EPA could make better use of science in its work. The committee members, for the most part, had not had direct experience within EPA. If their advice was to be useful, it had to be based on an understanding of the procedures and processes of the Agency, coupled with knowledge of the capabilities and resources that scientific research could contribute to the regulatory process. Members were experienced in various aspects of environmental science research and development, the management of technical organizations, and the

---

[1]Robert W. Berliner to Russell E. Train, August 27, 1974. Report of the Review Committee on the Management of the Research and Development Activities of the U.S. Environmental Protection Agency. (The Berliner Report: reproduced as Appendix C of Volume III, Research and Development in EPA. See Table 2 of this report.)

FIGURE 1 Structure of the NRC Program of Analytical Studies for the U.S. Environmental Protection Agency

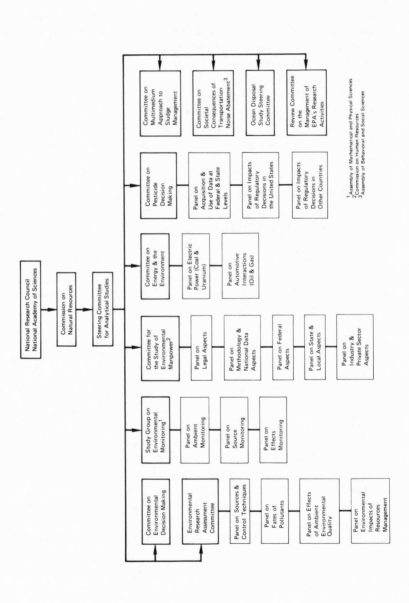

institutions, programs, and policies characteristic of the relationship between science and government.

The committees met with many EPA officials and were provided with documents pertinent to their inquiries. Interviews concerned with specific aspects of science and decision making were conducted with former EPA officials, other government officials at federal, state, and local levels, and leaders from industry and environmental groups. The staff studied past decisions chosen to illustrate the variety of circumstances in which scientific information is used. Committee members visited a number of EPA laboratories and observed field activities, including Regional Offices. More than 1000 people provided information. Two meetings were held between the chairmen of the component studies and the EPA Assistant Administrators. Descriptive material in working drafts of the reports was circulated within EPA to verify factual information. The Agency appointed staff persons to act as liaison to each study committee, to attend meetings (other than those where recommendations were deliberated), and to facilitate the provision of necessary information. In addition to the supporting material included in these reports, minutes of meetings, correspondence, and other documentation are available in the public access files of the National Research Council. A concise factual description of EPA and its current decision-making processes and procedures can be found in Appendixes A, B, and C of the report of the Committee on Environmental Decision Making.

THE CHANGING SCENE OF ENVIRONMENTAL REGULATION

The laws constituting the legislative authority of the Agency were passed at a time of mounting concern that technology and industry were damaging nature, human health, and the quality of life out of all proportion to short-term material benefits. At the same time, the public and Congress were disappointed by the failure of existing laws adequately to protect the environment through implementation largely by the states. An abrupt halt to the habitual misuse of air, water, and landscape was overdue.

The laws fixed ambitious goals and timetables for pollution abatement. Some gross and obvious pollution (such as particulate matter in air or untreated municipal sewage) was relatively easy to identify and to begin to remedy. Although data were sparse, the social and political judgment was that the benefits clearly exceeded the costs in these initial abatement activities, and the technology was available for substantial reduction of

TABLE 2 Titles of the Reports of the Committees and Panels of the NRC Program of Analytical Studies for the U.S. EPA

Vol. No.	Title of Report	Authors
I	Perspectives on Technical Information for Environmental Protection	Steering Committee for Analytical Studies and Commission on Natural Resources
II	Environmental Decision Making	Committee on Environmental Decision Making
III	Research and Development in EPA	Environmental Research Assessment Committee
IIIa	Sources of Residuals and Techniques for Their Control: Research and Development Needs*	Panel on Sources and Control Techniques
IIIb	Fates of Pollutants: Research and Development Needs*	Panel on Fates of Pollutants
IIIc	Effects of a Polluted Environment: Research and Development Needs*	Panel on Effects of Ambient Environmental Quality
IIId	Environmental Impacts of Resources Management: Research and Development Needs*	Panel on Environmental Impacts of Resources Management
IV	Environmental Monitoring	Study Group on Environmental Monitoring
		Panel on Ambient Monitoring
		Panel on Source Monitoring
		Panel on Effects Monitoring
V	Manpower for Environmental Pollution Control	Committee for Study of Environmental Manpower
	Appendix A: Legal Aspects of Manpower for Environmental Pollution Control	Panel on Legal Aspects
	Appendix B: Methodology and National Data Aspects of	Panel on Methodology and National Data Aspects

Appendix D: State and Local Aspects of Environmental Pollution Control Manpower	Panel on State and Local Aspects
Appendix E: Industry and Private Sector Aspects of Pollution Control Manpower	Panel on Industry and Private Sector Aspects
(These Appendixes are bound with the Committee Report in a single volume.)	
VI — Implications of Environmental Regulations for Energy Production and Consumption	Committee on Energy and the Environment
VII — Pesticide Decision Making	Committee on Pesticide Regulation
VIII — Multimedium Approach to Municipal Sludge Management	Committee on Multimedium Approach to Municipal Sludge Management
IX — Societal Consequences of Transportation Noise Abatement	Committee on Societal Consequences of Transportation Noise Abatement
X — Disposal in the Marine Environment (NRC 1976)	Committee on Disposal in the Marine Environment
XI — Review of Management of EPA's Research Activities (Bound with Volume III)	Review Committee on the Management of the Research and Development Activities of the U.S. Environmental Protection Agency

*Report is available from the NRC in limited number in multilith. Reports not marked with an asterisk can be purchased from the Printing and Publishing Office, National Academy of Sciences, 2101 Constitution Avenue, N.W., Washington, D.C. 20418.

effluents and emissions. Ambient air quality standards to protect some facets of human health were set on the basis of whatever data were available from clinical, epidemiological, and animal studies. Water quality could be improved, according to then prevailing views of safety, by rudimentary attention to sewage treatment and impoundment of toxic wastes. EPA was under stress to meet deadlines for the establishment of regulations and standards mandated by legislation.

But following this initial surge of activity, a broader, more difficult, more complex phase of environmental protection has begun. A number of toxic substances have been identified as air and water pollutants. Refinements in research and monitoring have revealed more subtle or unexpected impacts of exotic chemicals on ecosystems, frequently at low concentrations. Dramatic illustrations of the vulnerability of the environment have been provided by leaks, spills, and other pollution episodes. Interactions among pollutants (such as sulfur oxides and particulate matter) have emphasized the complex determinants of ambient environmental quality (see Chapter 2 of the report of the Committee on Energy and the Environment, referred to after this as *Energy*). It has been recognized that elimination of the last small traces of emissions and effluents can be very costly. Benefits have remained difficult to quantify, but continued investigation has suggested ever more extensive costs of damage to the environment and human health. Gaps in knowledge have continued to emerge.

Many environmental protection regulations impinge on land-use planning (for example, the control of indirect sources of air pollution, such as shopping centers that attract and concentrate automobile traffic, or the river basin planning associated with sewer systems and sewage treatment plant construction). The pervasive effect of air and water pollution control laws in planning and economic development has become apparent.

The range of technical information required for regulation encompasses virtually all fields of science. Alternative control technologies and strategies have to be compared for cost and effectiveness. Total elimination of pollutants is often not practicable and sometimes impossible. It has become important to be able to compare the extra costs and benefits associated with successively more stringent levels of control, increasing our need for knowledge of damages from pollution and costs of abatement.

The experience of the oil embargo of 1973–74 and the subsequent increase in the world price of oil has further complicated the problem of environmental protection. The long-term reliance on imported oil is questioned principally for reasons of national security, yet a turn to increased combustion of coal appears to be in direct conflict with air quality and land reclamation objectives. Despite the acknowledged strong impact on developments at certain sites using certain technologies, overall the portion of current energy costs assignable to environmental protection is in the range of 4 to 6 percent. The impact on future developments is more difficult to assess, but we conclude that it will remain a minor factor (see *Energy*, Chapter 1).

More generally, in the past two years, a slump in economic activity and employment has led some people to question environmental priorities. Business firms already pinched by low recession-level profits find pollution control costs a burden. In a time of weak markets, they cannot easily pass those costs on to the consumer who must, except perhaps in the short run, bear them. Some old and small plants have closed because their chronically lean profits were finally eliminated by the costs of pollution control requirements. Although new jobs and business opportunities have been created in fields related to environmental improvements, displaced workers and businesses can hardly hope to avoid prolonged losses in a depressed economy. It is important to keep in mind that these losses are primarily costs of recession; but the circumstances are not calculated to make pollution control universally popular.

Finally, the public has shown increased antipathy toward governmental regulations of all kinds. The intrusion into private activities, the apparently senseless paperwork, the perception of a distant bureaucracy unaware of local needs, and the real or apparent arbitrariness and capriciousness of some regulatory actions have bred a skepticism that has contaminated environmental issues as well.

The changing scene in which environmental regulation takes place has made the task of EPA more difficult. The National Research Council studies have therefore concentrated on the current situation instead of a detailed retrospective examination of the way scientific and technical information was used in the Agency's early years. The immediate future will see continuation of the trend to increasingly complex and poorly understood cause-and-effect relationships, the need for careful balancing among costs and benefits, and debate over national priorities.

The members of the study groups have found no valid reason to question the essential rightness of the national commitment to environmental management and improvement that gave rise to EPA in the first place. The difficulties of the newer phase are in part inevitable, as easier problems are dealt with before harder problems, and in part extraneous to EPA itself. The recommendations in this series of reports are designed to help EPA derive greatest benefit from the resources of science under these difficult conditions.

2 The Role of Scientific and Technical Information in Environmental Regulatory Decision Making

The protection of environmental quality must be made consistent with many other objectives of society, such as the industrial use of natural resources and the achievement of equity among groups and regions. Balancing these sometimes conflicting goals is a political process in which the information derived from scientific investigations plays only one part. The National Research Council study of the EPA decision-making process and of a number of regulations suggests that nontechnical factors often dominate environmental issues. Technical factors define the problem and determine what is feasible and what it will cost, but hardly ever will they alone determine what is desirable. Subjective judgments about institutional capabilities and political acceptability must be integrated with scientific and technical information by government administrators. Indeed, in a democracy, hard decisions about clashing interests should be reached openly, not abdicated to a "technocracy."

The question remains whether EPA is generating, acquiring, and using technical information to the full extent that the Agency properly needs and that the state of knowledge allows. The National Research Council studies suggest that efficiency of acquisition and credibility in use will both be increased to the extent that the Agency's scientific activities are: (1) responsive to regulatory needs (see Chapter 1 of the report of the Environmental Research Assessment Committee, referred to after this as *Research*; and Chapter 3 of the report of the Committee on Environmental Decision Making, referred to after this as *Decision Making*); (2) attentive to problems of implementation (*Research*, Chapter 5) and enforcement; (3) coordinated with the research, development, and monitoring of other agencies (*Research*, Chapter 1; and Chapter 4 of the report of the Study Group on Environmental Monitoring, referred to after this as *Monitoring*); (4) planned, performed, and validated with appropriate and timely participation from the scientific and engineering community (*Research*, Chapter 4; *Decision Making*, Chapter 3; and *Monitoring*, Chapter 4); and (5) explicit, public, and fully reported in advance of the time that regulations are promulgated (*Decision Making*, Chapters 2 and 4; *Research*, Chapter 4; NRC 1975b). Furthermore, the Environmental Research Assessment Committee is convinced by its analysis that the management of the Agency's research and development should be centralized in the Office of Research and Development. A significant advantage would be the integration of research concerning impacts on air, land, and water—integration that is difficult when the work is performed to meet the specific interests of one program office. The Study Group on Environmental Monitoring also suggests the development of an Office of Science to assure that scientific principles are integrated into Agency programs, particularly the design, operation, and evaluation of monitoring programs (*Monitoring*, Chapter 4). These studies agree that scientific leadership in the Agency should be strengthened at the highest levels of its administration. Alternative means are suggested and no attempt is made to reconcile them into a specific, single organizational design.

THE INTRINSIC UNCERTAINTY OF SCIENCE

Some of the difficulties of environmental management are inherent in the nature of environmental systems. Many different organisms, including human beings, interact with the physical environment through flows of energy and materials. The structure of most natural and man-influenced ecosystems is both complex and characterized by natural oscillations in abundance and interactions among constituent species as well as by various changes in environmental conditions. Natural variability may make it difficult, even after careful study of a particular ecosystem, to characterize in a dependable fashion what changes will result from a particular environmental assault on the system. Complicating this state of affairs is the fact that almost none of the earth's ecosystems is now known or understood in substantial detail. Thus, in many cases we simply do not know the full consequences of a proposed regulatory decision or of a decision not to act at all (see Chapter 5 of the report of the Committee on Multimedium Approach to Municipal Sludge Management, referred to after this as *Sludge,* and Chapter 3 of the report of the Committee on Disposal in the Marine Environment, referred to after this as *Disposal*).

The uncertainties and incompleteness of environmental science, when candidly admitted, are frustrating; but it is unrealistic and improper for the politically responsible decision maker to expect and demand more than science can provide. It is equally improper for technical analysts to fail to explain clearly the limits of their knowledge, the margin of uncertainty in their estimates, and the gaps that might be closed by further research.

Two kinds of judgment are involved in EPA decision making; cognitive judgment based on scientific information and analyses, and evaluative judgment based on policy considerations. The two are often confused and mixed, reflecting, in part, a failure of communication between the technical and political communities. Cognitive judgments are subject to review and validation by the scientific community. Evaluative judgments as to how best to achieve the goals of policy, or to set priorities among competing goals, must always remain in the political arena for final appraisal. For example, the identification and assessment of risks to ecosystems or human health are the responsibility of science, but the determination of the acceptability of a risk is a task for the political process. It is often impossible to separate these two kinds of judgments completely, but that is not a reason for failing to try.

The more systematic analysis recommended in *Decision Making* (Chapter 2) and the integrated technical analysis recommended in *Research* (Chapter 2) would help to clarify the usefulness of scientific and technical information.

Although EPA's elaborate procedures for developing standards and regulations have significantly improved the quality of analysis by assuring open review of proposed actions, the analysis nevertheless often treats important factors inadequately. In its current decision-making processes, the Agency does not consistently include a systematic and comprehensive consideration of feasible alternatives.

EPA's decisions on standards and regulations should be supported by analyses that explictly state the objectives of the decisions, identify feasible alternatives, evaluate (quantitatively, to the extent possible) the consequences of each alternative decision, explore potential problems in implementation, and indicate and examine the degree of uncertainty about the effects of EPA actions. The analyses should be available to the public. (*Decision Making,* Chapter 2, and Appendix D, which describes methods of analysis.)

Assessment of available data begins with the collection of physical, chemical, statistical, biological, economic, social, and technological data from existing sources. The data are then analyzed for accuracy and relevance, and synthesized and interpreted in terms suggested by the people who will use the results. To be useful to decision makers for the task of assessing available options, the analyses must organize the information in a form that clearly defines relationships among different aspects of a problem and places the data on each aspect (for example, a health hazard) in the context of the overall framework of human interaction with the environment. Limits of confidence in the data and uncertainties in the analyses must be stated explicitly . . . . The results of such analyses may also be used to identify critical research needs, and thus would also be useful for planning research activities in EPA. (*Research*, Chapter 2.)

In evaluating the benefits to be gained from the reduction of a particular pollutant, heavy weight is usually given to the statistical evidence of economic effects. To place a money value on a variety of social, physiological, and psychological effects is difficult and unsettling, but desirable in order to have benefit estimates that can be compared with costs. Such judgments are in fact made in many instances, though usually implicitly. It is important that research be undertaken in the design and testing of more direct or alternative measures of these benefits. Both with economic measures and with any alternatives that can be designed and validated, attention should be given to the distribution of benefits (and costs) as well as the total amount (*Research*, Chapter 2).

FUNCTIONS OF EPA AND THE ROLE OF INFORMATION

Environmental legislation affects the missions of other agencies of government—such as the Federal Energy Administration, the Department of Defense, the U.S. Department of Agriculture, and the Department of Transportation—and is but one ingredient in national policy, along with economic growth, national security, food and energy supply, and other factors. In administering federal environmental policy, EPA is thus sometimes cast in the role of antagonist, in opposition not only to those who are to be regulated but to other government agencies, like the Corps of Engineers in the case of ocean disposal regulations (*Disposal*, Chapter 3).

In several of the laws that EPA administers (such as the Clean Air Act and the Federal Water Pollution Control Act), the Congressional decision to regulate included a specification of the form that the regulations were to take. All that remained for EPA was to set standards and enforce them. In these cases, EPA's posture as both protagonist and regulator inevitably reflects upon the role the Agency accords to scientific information. At the outset a case is to be made: a regulation and a certain degree of stringency in standards are to be supported. Information that might undermine support may not be sought with sufficient ardor, the risk of antagonizing some sources of information may be avoided, and analysis and interpretation may be colored by an emphasis on the protective mission.

In other contexts (such as regulating a pesticide, a toxic substance, or noise) EPA must decide, within the flexibility permitted by the law, whether to regulate or not, and, if it does, to what extent; the decision must be based on a full exploration of benefits and costs of control. In these situations, the Agency's information gathering will be more comprehensive. The balancing function is the duty of the EPA Administrator.

Another role for EPA is public education. Successful and equitable control of pollution depends ultimately on public understanding and acceptance of the costs and possible changes in lifestyle necessary to achieve it. Among the many sources of information available to the public, the federal government is inevitably an important one and it should warrant a high degree of credibility.

This consideration also emphasizes the need for monitoring the status and trends of environmental quality. Reliable, consistent, and timely reporting on the quality of air, water, and ecosystems is required for judging the progress of federal programs and setting priorities for future action (*Monitoring*, Chapter 2). Well-planned, basic monitoring information of good quality is an essential ingredient of control strategy, determining relationshps among sources of pollution, ambient environmental quality, and effects on humans, animals, and plants; and discovering environmental problems by keeping watch on trends in ambient environmental quality and responses to changes.

The publication of status and trend reports by the Council on Environmental Quality as mandated by NEPA can combine the monitoring information from EPA with that of several other agencies in a comprehensive annual review.

EPA also reviews Environmental Impact Statements (EIS) prepared by other units of government. It interacts with the state and local governments that must implement and enforce many regulations established at the federal level. These enforcement levels should be a source to EPA of much valuable information, and these government units depend in turn on the Agency for complete and timely information to support their implementation plans.

THE PROCESS OF ACQUISITION

EPA procedures allow and encourage the continuous introduction of knowledge from the initial intent to set regulations to the adjudication of specific environmental protection actions. The process is open; and highly motivated participation of EPA, other government agencies, industry, and public interest groups works toward full elucidation of the issues.

The data and theories of science will usually have been reviewed and validated by discussion, inspection, and replication in the tradition of the scientific method. In addition, the information in science archives is organized for retrieval in a way that facilitates bringing to the surface any existing information in the published scientific literature relevant to an EPA decision.

A different source of existing information, however, is proprietary or otherwise unpublished data. Equitable regulations require an under-standing of the processes of industrial manufacturing, the efficacy and toxicity of products, and the technological feasibility of abatement. Partly by necessity and partly because of its own limited research capabilities, EPA now relies on the regulated industries themselves for much of this information. The resulting problem of credibility is apparent. Remedial recommendations include both the strengthening of EPA's own research and validation programs, including certification of laboratory perfor-mance (*Research*, Chapters 4 and 5; *Monitoring*, Chapter 3; and *Decision Making*, Chapter 3) and the systematic review, using scientists both inside and outside EPA, of information submitted by interested parties (*Decision Making*, Chapter 3).

In addition to existing information, much new data for special purposes must be generated by research and monitoring. EPA supports, in its own laboratories and by contract with outside performers, about one-seventh of all the federal research and development in environmental science and engineering (*Research*, Chapter 1). But EPA's formal research effort—budgeted in FY 1978 at about $266 million—cannot provide all the data the Agency needs in support of regulations. Priorities in EPA research are inevitably affected by external events (such as Congressional mandates, pollution episodes, or industrial emergencies) at some cost to systematic, long-term planning.

The National Research Council studies support the current emphasis of EPA research in support of decision making. EPA is a regulatory agency; it does not have sole responsibility for scientific progress in the diverse fields of environmental research. Yet, undoubtedly, some amount of EPA research should be dedicated with continuity to long-range, fundamental investigation. This research is necessary to understand ecosystems, to improve monitoring, and to develop a capability for anticipating environmental impacts. A specific legislative mandate to perform some research independent of support for pollution control regulations is recommended (*Research*, Chapter 1).

A second aspect of current EPA research and monitoring is that coordination with other federal agencies is important to enhance prompt transfer into the regulatory process of research results generated elsewhere (*Research*, Chapter 1; *Monitoring*, Chapter 4; and Chapter 3 of the report of the Committee on Societal Consequences of Transportation Noise Abatement, referred to after this as *Noise*). Coordination in planning research is difficult because each agency must first fulfill its own mission. An interagency transfer of funds from EPA is one means of obtaining information from the research arm of another agency. Because of the number of agencies involved and the diversity of research applicable to environmental problems, the Office of Science and Technology Policy and the Office of Management and Budget should assist in insuring the required interagency cooperation by assigning responsibilities and allocating resources (*Research*, Chapter 1).

A valuable adjunct to the acquisition process is the initiative of scientists outside the federal establishment in bringing innovations and discoveries into governmental activity. As yet, however, the scientific community and its established institutions do not identify closely enough with EPA's mission and activities. Many older government agencies, through a long history of support of training and research, have developed rapport with large numbers of scientists. In these cases, there is a ready and continuous interchange of information about government problems and the state of knowledge in various fields. Efficient regulations to protect the environment will depend, increasingly, on sophisticated understanding of the movement of pollutants through the biosphere and their subtle effects on human health and ecosystems. Ideas about solving the most perplexing pollution problems and inventions to make the ideas work must come from such a variety of scientific research and field investigations that no reasonable budget and research plan of EPA's alone could cover all the possibilities.

Information and data assembled within EPA would gain in authority and reliability through closer ties with the outside scientific community. The National Research Council reports recommend that the whole EPA research program, from the planning of investigations to the publication of results, interact more closely with outside scientists and scientific institutions (see *Decision Making*, Chapter 3; *Research*, Chapter 4; and *Monitoring*, Chapters 3 and 4).

It is the consensus of these studies that EPA has not used, in a fully effective way, the experience and judgment available throughout the scientific community. The reasons include unrealistic deadlines set by Congress and the resulting impatience on the part of some EPA staff, indifference of some nongovernment scientists, and inadequately planned research programs and poorly defined missions of laboratories inherited by EPA. The scientific activities of the Agency have been too isolated from the critical evaluation of experienced professionals in other agencies and in the academic and industrial communities.

The Agency should systematically build familiarity with its program among leading nonfederal scientists and institutions by judicious funding of training grants and research. (See *Research,* Chapters 3 and 4, for recommendations on how to accomplish this goal.)

EPA's Science Advisory Board (SAB) offers excellent promise for participation by nongovernment scientists and engineers in EPA's programs. The SAB has recently become fully activated, and its effectiveness will develop only over a considerable period of time. The extent to which the SAB is used is at the discretion of the Administrator since it is not established by law. Two hazards are apparent: the SAB could eventually lose its independence and credibility if it were to be co-opted by the Agency; or the Board might antagonize EPA management and lose any influence in the operation of the Agency's science program. A strengthened and more stable SAB (see *Decision Making,* Chapter 3), with the ability to take the initiative in scientific issues, could help to channel outside scientific advice to the Administrator.

THE USE OF SCIENTIFIC INFORMATION

Environmental regulation is not a detached, leisurely process of transforming verified results of objective scientific research into clearly indicated regulatory decisions. Nor will it ever be. The timing and the content of EPA's regulatory decisions are bound to be controversial. Powerful interests are involved. The proponents of quick and stringent regulation regard delay and compromise as tantamount to trifling with health, welfare, and the survival of environmental amenity. Those about to be regulated see regulation as a threat to their livelihood or property and a hasty surrender to uninformed outsiders. The Agency is attacked from both sides by litigious parties at interest convinced of the rightness of their cause.

At the heart of much reaction to regulations from industry and the public is a stout belief in the English Common Law concept that a person is "innocent until proven guilty" and that the burden of proof rests with the accuser. However, identified risks to environmental values and human health (from existing or proposed technology) often imply severe damage, irreversible change, or long delayed consequences of a sort that makes it appropriate for the technology's proponent to bear additional responsibility at least in furnishing information about possible unwanted effects. More than merely shifting the burden of proof, this responsibility calls for anticipation and assessment of impacts of technological change more broadly and over a longer time than has been required up to now. These concepts are now embodied in the Federal Insecticide, Fungicide and Rodenticide Act (amended) and the Toxic Substances Control Act.

Confrontation and the adversary process do not create an atmosphere conducive to the careful weighing of scientific and technical evidence. Much information introduced in the process of regulation is suspected by one side of having been tailored to make a case for the other. Even the credibility of research performed for and by EPA is weakened because the Agency itself appears as a party at interest, especially in litigation.

If there were no time pressure in the regulatory process, the normal accumulation and validation of scientific knowledge would eventually dissipate much controversy. Scientific evidence would be subject to critical review by the appropriate professional community. Experiments would be replicated, alternative hypotheses explored and tested, and technical judgments checked against established theory and one or the other amended as necessary. Eventually the technical basis for decision making would emerge with greater clarity.

But regulatory decision making is hurried by the real or imagined urgency of environmental problems, by public demands for action, and by the resulting statutory deadlines. Congress and EPA are often forced to act before there is sufficient reliable scientific basis for action. This rush to regulate is not necessarily wrong: the decision not to regulate is also a decision. If there is no adequate scientific–technical basis for regulation, neither is there an adequate scientific–technical basis for the belief that no regulation is needed. The danger is that, under the pressure of adversary interests, the methods of science are bent, and tentative research results may be presented as proven fact.

The Committee on Environmental Decision Making recommends:

Scientific and technical data and analyses used in decision making should be reviewed routinely at an early stage to assure that all relevant data are considered and to reduce the possibility of misinterpretation or misuse of scientific results. In this process EPA will be greatly aided by the wide range of scientific and engineering expertise that exists outside the Agency. The reviews should be available to the public as a matter of course.

On decisions that set significant precedents or have a substantial impact on public health or welfare or on public or private expenditures, the Administrator personally should have access to independent scientific advice and evaluations of the technical basis for decisions. This can best be accomplished by increasing the responsibilities of the existing Science Advisory Board (SAB) so that its chairman would serve full time for a fixed term and would convey independent evaluations of scientific and technical data and analyses directly to the Administrator.

(*Decision Making*, Chapter 3).

EPA already does in isolated instances what the National Research Council studies now suggest it should do regularly. Costs, risks, and benefits are to be identified in the case of pesticides, but not elsewhere; decision papers are now occasionally published as preambles to Proposed Regulations published in the Federal Register, as in the case of the vinyl chloride regulations, but not in all cases. The process should be extended and made general. The advantages of open and explicit analysis of the basis for regulatory decisions are illustrated in specific instances in several of the committee reports. (See, for example, *Energy*, Chapter 3; *Sludge*, Chapter 4; and *Noise*, Chapter 8.)

MONITORING

The National Research Council studies pay special attention to EPA's role as a producer and consumer of primary information about the environment. Monitoring activities are obviously indispensable to regulation. Sources of pollution must be monitored to verify compliance with standards or, in some regulatory systems, to measure appropriate penalties. The monitoring of ambient environmental quality is essential to the Agency in knowing whether regulation is having the intended effect, and in establishing baselines against which to measure changes in environmental quality and thereby to assess trends and anticipate problems. Measuring the responses of humans, animals, and plants and relating these measurements to environmental quality is important for understanding the effects of pollution, and thus the benefits of abatement.

Monitoring for compliance is part of the day-to-day enforcement operations of the Agency. Monitoring of the effects of pollution and the condition of the ambient environment are longer-term efforts of the Agency that achieve their full value only when they are conducted in compatible ways over long periods of time. Such monitoring provides the foundations of integrated technical analysis. It is our judgment that the nation's information on environmental quality is deplorably and unnecessarily bad.

Direct observation is only part of the monitoring effort. Massive bodies of data have to be analyzed, reduced to manageable information, preferably with known statistical properties, and then made available to decision makers.

The Study Group on Environmental Monitoring (SGEM) finds current monitoring deficient in three major ways (see *Monitoring*, Chapter 2). First, scientific principles are used inadequately in the design, operation, and evaluation of monitoring programs, even within the Agency. As a result, current monitoring does not adequately serve the important purposes of evaluating the progress of national environmental programs in terms of improved environmental quality and of determining relationships among sources of pollution, ambient environmental quality, and effects on humans, animals, and plants. Second, there is an imbalance in EPA's emphasis on monitoring for controlling sources of pollution rather than for anticipating and discovering environmental problems (see also *Research*, Chapter 2). The Agency should monitor the responses of humans, animals, and plants to changes in environmental quality; and it should monitor to forecast pollution problems so that they can be, at best, prevented or, at least, diminished in effect. EPA established monitoring programs at great speed to meet exigencies of pollution control. Thus, we have important gaps in environmental monitoring and, at the same time, a proliferation of monitoring programs that are inefficient, inflexible, and productive of data of poor or unknown quality. The SGEM concludes that a central reason for these problems is the lack of scientific leadership: science is inadequately brought to bear on the operation of EPA programs. The SGEM recommends that EPA further develop its own scientific capabilities so that it can attain scientific leadership, particularly in the design of monitoring networks and in other sciences of environmental monitoring. In addition, special emphasis should be placed on the development and evaluation of direct and indirect techniques for monitoring individual sources of air and water pollution. Improvement of source monitoring is important for enforcing compliance with regulations or with the levying of regulatory charges.

Third, monitoring is fragmented (see *Monitoring*, Chapter 4). There is inadequate coordination among local, state, regional, and federal agencies, and even among programs within EPA itself. Some measurement systems overlap wastefully, and some data are collected that cannot be properly used because other data are not collected. Some of the fragmentation is mandated by law, because Congress included excessively detailed specification for data collection in the various acts administered by EPA. This situation should be corrected along with other consequences of legislative fragmentation discussed in Chapter 3 of this perspectives report. SGEM recommends that EPA work with the state, local, and other federal agencies to make current monitoring activities mutually compatible so that, taken together, they form a national system (*Monitoring*, Chapter 4). To coordinate federal environmental monitoring efforts, particularly so that data on environmental quality can be related to data on health and ecological effects, SGEM recommends that a National Committee on Environmental Monitoring be established (*Monitoring*, Chapter 4). Similarly, it is the judgment of ERAC that, because of the necessary participation in monitoring of several federal, state, regional, and local agencies and private parties, leadership at the level of the Executive Office of the President is required. The responsibility would rest most appropriately in the Office of Science and Technology Policy (*Research*, Chapter 2).

MANPOWER IN THE REGULATORY PROCESS

It is axiomatic that an agency involved in a field as technically complex as the environment cannot function without an adequate supply of people highly skilled in science. Indeed, quite apart from EPA, the whole system—the regulated as well as the regulators, the private sector and state and local governments—requires the services of technically trained people. For this reason, an entire study was devoted to environmental manpower (see Volume V of the series, the report of the Committee for Study of Environmental Manpower, referred to after this as *Manpower*).

The Committee for Study of Environmental Manpower (CSEM) found no reason to expect a large-scale shortage of skilled manpower nationwide in the environmental field, but several deficiencies in the system surfaced in the course of the Committee's investigation.

It is a general conclusion of CEDM that the Congressional policy of setting timetables for regulatory action is an effective incentive to action (see *Decision Making*, Chapter 3). However, where the labor market is involved, the resulting lead times are often too short for the market to produce in its traditional way an adequate supply of qualified people to operate the programs. It follows that manpower considerations should play an explicit role when legislation is drafted, and not just after legislation has been enacted and the regulatory process has begun.

CSEM believes that EPA can and should assume responsibility for assuring its own supply of qualified people. In particular, the association of training activities with the Agency's own research activities might be made to yield a dividend in trained manpower to operate the technical aspects of pollution control programs.

Although most training of qualified environmental personnel will naturally fall to educational institutions and industrial training programs, CSEM recommends that EPA take the lead in projecting national trends in the supply and demand for technically trained people, in coordinating a federal manpower program for environmental control, and in providing technical assistance to lower levels of government. Funds should be allocated to educational institutions on a continuing basis for the development of research and training centers (see also *Research*, Chapter 3). This effort should also consider the retraining of chemists, physicists, and other scientists in environmental specialties.

CSEM expressed some doubts about whether, aside from any considerations of competence, EPA's technical staff is being properly used. In particular, there appear to be too few technically trained people with experience in pollution control at decision-making levels (see also the report of the Committee on Pesticide Decision Making, referred to after this as *Pesticides*). It has already been pointed out that technical considerations are central but will rarely be decisive in the making of environmental policy; but the correct interpretation and application of scientific and technical information in the regulatory process would be facilitated if appropriately trained, experienced people in EPA were involved throughout that process. In particular, the leaders of the Office of Research and Development should be respected environmental scientists as well as good administrators (*Research*, Chapter 4).

3 Opportunities for Congressional Action

Our laws dealing with natural resources and the environment have been established over many years for diverse purposes of exploitation and regulation. As a set, these laws are not always internally consistent as guiding policies, and their statutes are often in conflict with other laws concerning other national goals, such as full employment, public health, and national security. This ambiguity of national policies is neither surprising nor completely avoidable in a changing and diverse society. Priorities are established from time to time, and the implementation of specific laws is necessarily adjusted to current public opinion. Nevertheless, greater consistency among environmental laws appears desirable for improved management, and some outright conflicts in laws are frustrating the efficient protection of the environment.

Three levels or degrees of inclusiveness may be visualized. In the broadest sense, it would be desirable to include all relevant aspects of natural resources use and land-use planning, since environmental quality is a result of the complete system of extraction, processing, consumption, and disposal of fuels and materials. The provision of the National Environmental Policy Act requiring the preparation and use of Environmental Impact Statements in major and significant federal activities seeks to achieve this broad comprehension. The need to prepare the EIS has increased the amount of information available to all interested parties and has contributed to decisions based to a greater extent upon a balancing of national objectives.

In a somewhat more restricted sense, the laws concerning all aspects of environmental quality could and should be made more consistent and compatible. Environmental quality is closely related to land-use planning, urbanization, economic development, and population policy. At present, because of the conflicting objectives and priorities expressed in legislation, it is unclear which policies should prevail when conflicts occur, or how attempts should be made to reconcile conflicting objectives. Aside from EPA, many agencies (both developmental and regulatory) have functions that deal with the quality of the environment; e.g., the Fish and Wildlife Service, the Corps of Engineers, the National Oceanic and Atmospheric Administration, the National Parks Service, the Occupational Safety and Health Administration, the Nuclear Regulatory Commission, the Food and Drug Administration, and others. The acceptable level of risk to environmental values and human health varies widely as evaluated by different agencies. A balanced allocation of public funds and administrative emphasis is difficult to achieve.

An even more restricted level of comprehensiveness is that of pollution abatement and control—the primary mission of EPA and the focus of the National Research Council studies. While the analyses of the studies provide ample evidence of the need for coordination of legislation at all levels, it is particularly important that the laws regulating pollution be more consistent and coherent.

The basis for a more consistent set of environmental laws should be the technical nature of environmental problems. For example, management of ambient environmental quality—whether of the air, land, or water, and whether by standard setting and enforcement of regulations or some other strategy—should be treated consistently. They are one and the same problem, expressed in different media. Legislation aimed at achieving and maintaining environmental quality may have to be supplemented by consistent legislation designed specifically to protect human health and welfare against substances in the environment that may be toxic even in small concentrations. The Federal Insecticide, Fungicide, and Rodenticide Act and the Toxic Substances Control Act, for example, are designed for such protection.

THE FRAGMENTING EFFECTS OF CURRENT LAWS

The Legislative and Executive documents concerning the organization of the Environmental Protection Agency in 1970 clearly accept the interdependencies among components of the environment. Presidents, Congressional leaders, Administrators of EPA, and a host of commentators from the private sector have all emphasized that the rationale for the new agency has been to bring together the once separate pollution control programs and organize a unified, balanced effort to clean up the air, the water, and the landscape to protect human health and welfare. EPA was to perform a systematic identification of all pollutants; trace their movement through the media of air, water, soil, and organism; determine permissible levels of exposure for human beings and ecosystems; and control pollution so that one part of the environment is not improved in quality at excessive cost to another part. To accomplish these objectives, research, standard setting, and enforcement would have to occur comprehensively.

But no new authority was given to EPA: the Agency was merely made responsible for a set of existing laws governing air pollution, water pollution, solid wastes, pesticides, and radiation. EPA was not required to prepare Environmental Impact Statements on its own regulatory actions—a function that could have directed attention to a wider variety of environmental considerations, such as land-use planning. (In 1975, the Agency began voluntarily to prepare Environmental Impact Statements on some of its major decisions.) The Council on Environmental Quality was to perform a coordinating and advisory role relative to all federal programs dealing with the environment, but the Council was given no "line" authority to enforce a balance among pollution abatement programs.

Since the establishment of EPA, Congress has continued to enact additional laws to restore and enhance environmental quality. These laws are also narrow in purpose and are not integrated with one another or with previous laws to allow comprehensive implementation (see *Sludge*, Chapter 5). The 1972 Amendments to the Federal Water Pollution Control Act do call for an analysis of "the total economic, social, and environmental effects of achieving or not achieving" the pollution control goals, but the National Commission on Water Quality, not EPA, was to perform this task.

EPA was first organized along functional lines of standard setting, enforcement, and research. Soon the organization was changed to a mixture of functions with program areas in air and water. The Agency management attempts to review major regulatory decisions for their effects on all media, but the constraints of Congressional mandates prevent systematic balancing, and the review most often occurs only after regulation has been developed.

Our current pollution control laws do not adequately take into account interconnections among the various environmental disposal media. The fragmentation results in inefficient, confusing, and sometimes counter-productive regulatory decisions by EPA.

The study of the management of municipal sewage treatment plant sludge illustrates the complexities that arise when a given residual material that may be placed in or on land or water or in air falls under the purview of several environmental laws (*Sludge*, Chapter 5). In an effort to protect the fresh waters of the country, Public Law 92-500 mandates certain levels of wastewater treatment. A consequence of that national goal is the production of increasing amounts of sludge, while other federal legislation restricts management options for the material. For example, the Marine Protection, Research, and Sanctuaries Act (PL 92-532) has been interpreted by the Administrator of EPA as a prohibition of ocean dumping of municipal sludge. Similarly the Clean Air Act Amendments of 1970 may restrict use of sludge incinerators. Each of these acts is directed toward protecting individual sectors of the environment. However, the land is not currently accorded similar federal protection and may therefore assume a greater burden as a disposal site in the future. At present individual sludge management plans must be formulated against a background of multiple jurisdictions residing in several units of the Agency. Without a rapid and coordinated Agency response to individual plans, there will continue to be problems with the timeliness, cost effectiveness, and overall environmental suitability of Agency actions.

Other examples of noncomprehensive regulation include: the stringent control of thermal pollution of waterways leading to use of cooling towers with their possible adverse impacts on aesthetic quality and local meteorological conditions; collection of particles from stack gases resulting in a loss of their neutralizing action and a subsequent increase in the acidity of rainfall; accumulation of sulfate sludge from the installation of sulfur oxide scrubbers; increased energy requirements for the removal of the last increments of effluents and emissions; and the exclusion of nonpoint sources, such as runoff from farms, from the strategy for improving water quality.

The current legislation also establishes timetables for various aspects of pollution control that are sometimes inconsistent with optimum management of the environment. For example, the introduction of new automobile engine technology appears to have been hampered by mandated emission standards and the timetable for their achievement; the catalytic converter added to existing engines was the only technically feasible means of compliance (see *Energy*; Chapter 3, and NRC 1975c). Another example is the dilemma created by having to achieve mandated deadlines for meeting air quality standards in regions where natural sources of pollutants are significant or where technology and other resources are not adequate to do so. A third example is the river basin planning program which will be completed only after the construction of many sewage treatment plants whose proper use and location ought to be determined by the plan. Nevertheless, we conclude that, on balance, the imposition of statutory deadlines for EPA action has been beneficial, perhaps necessary, and should continue (see *Decision Making*, Chapter 3). If legislation allowed or required a more comprehensive approach to environmental regulation, the deadlines would presumably mesh better and be more nearly consistent with efficient management of the environment.

Other requirements embodied in legislation need to be justified in a more comprehensive context than that in which they were enacted. For example, the Clean Air Act assumes that there is a threshold of toxicity that makes it feasible to set an ambient air quality standard to protect the health of all persons, and that this protection should be achieved regardless of cost. Another example is the requirement that nationwide uniform emission standards should lead to desired ambient air and water quality despite regional diversities as to meteorology, topography, and natural background conditions. The first of these examples, obviously, was a decision based not on scientific principle but on social and political considerations. The second was also founded on sound political principles, but it did not recognize the scientific fact that environmental conditions vary widely throughout this large country.

The control of pollution in air and water cannot be separated from consideration of land use. EPA's mandate "to preserve and enhance the Nation's air quality" has been interpreted as a prohibition against degradation of air quality. Such a requirement can be a powerful determinant in decisions on industrial siting, urban development, and other uses of land.

The Clean Air Amendments of 1970 contain two other examples of air pollution controls relating to land use: control of urban transportation and control of the location of indirect sources—such as shopping centers or stadiums that attract heavy traffic.

The most important features of the water quality law for land-use planning are the area plans required by Section 208 which establishes programs to control location, modification, and construction of all facilities that may discharge pollution.

Section 201 of the Water Pollution Control Act Amendments authorizes the Administrator of EPA to make grants for planning and construction of publicly owned sewage treatment plants. These construction grants have enormous implications for land development since, in large measure, the size and location of sewage treatment facilities along with interceptor sewer lines determine the shape and extent of community growth.

These examples illustrate the overlapping and at times contradictory effects of air and water pollution control laws and the effects of these laws on land use. Conversely, they show that land use can be a prime determinant of the nature and extent of air and water pollution.

Finally, the current legislation does not consider alternative strategies for achieving improved environmental quality. There may be cases where provision of economic incentives would be superior to conventional regulation in abating pollution. Examples are analyzed in the reports on *Noise* (Chapter 3), *Decision Making* (Chapter 6), *Sludge* (Chapters 4 and 5), and *Energy* (Chapter 4).

It may be asked why the fragmenting effect of pollution control laws has not been recognized and corrected up to this time. EPA could have suggested remedial legislation, but perhaps it is unrealistic to expect a young agency to go to Congress with complaints about the laws it is to administer. Such action, particularly in the atmosphere of partisan politics in Congress–White House relations of the recent past, would be likely to have led to sharp criticism of the Agency rather than to careful consideration of the inconsistencies and conflicts in the laws. However, it is appropriate and necessary for EPA to inform Congress about problems the Agency faces in implementing the laws it is called upon to administer. Congress itself cannot easily achieve a coordinated overview, because the various environmental laws are in the purview of different committees and subcommittees in both houses. These groups, in guarding their jurisdictions, tend to see pollution abatement from special standpoints.

The constraints of the set of pollution control laws are serious obstacles to efficient and equitable achievement of improved environmental quality. Leadership and candor in both these branches of government will be needed to design amendments and additional legislation to reconcile these conflicts.

ALTERNATIVE STRATEGIES FOR ACHIEVING ENVIRONMENTAL QUALITY

The various statutes administered by EPA lay down a particular approach to environmental regulation. In most cases, the law itself sets or requires the Agency to set minimum standards for the emission of certain pollutants along with timetables for their achievement. In other cases the legal requirement is specified in (rather vague) technological terms. A third possible approach, the use of economic incentives, would, as we have seen, have important advantages in some circumstances, but it has been excluded thus far from our environmental regulatory options (Kneese and Schultze 1975).

From one point of view, it makes no difference whether EPA is empowered to say, "Thou shalt not emit more than so much SO_x"; or to say, "For every bit of SO_x emitted, thou shalt pay so many cents." In principle, the same goals can be achieved either way. It is costly for businesses and households to meet emission standards, and more costly the more stringent the standard. They can be induced to meet any given standard by a regulatory charge that makes it more expensive not to meet it. So environmental goals can be met either way.

Nevertheless, the regulatory charge has some advantages that will, in certain circumstances, make it preferable to the emission standard. Most of the time, society's interest is to reduce the aggregate amount of pollution; the fraction of the total contributed by each potential polluter is of little or no importance. When that is so, the goal should be to achieve the desired level of environmental quality at lowest possible cost. If emission standards are set, then in practice the standard must be the same for each polluter. EPA cannot hope to have the information it would need in order to set more stringent standards for those businesses and households that happen to have low abatement costs, for reasons of technology, location, or accident, and less stringent standards for those who would find it extraordinarily costly to reduce their emissions. Yet that is clearly what needs to be done if the total cost of abatement is to be reduced. And, in principle, it can be done by the expedient of setting a regulatory charge and leaving the ultimate responses to each family and firm. Those with low abatement costs will find it cheaper to abate than to pay; those with high abatement costs will find it cheaper to pay than abate.

This example illustrates a second general advantage of the economic-incentive approach to environmental management. It has already been observed that much of the technical (and economic) information underlying sensible environmental control belongs naturally to the industries being regulated. EPA must and can acquire some of it for regulatory purposes, but it is obviously impossible to centralize all the relevant information in a regulatory agency. The economic-incentive approach permits EPA to reduce the cost of achieving a given level of environmental quality without having all the information; since the self-interested reactions of the regulated industries form part of the system of regulation, underlying knowledge of the technology and economics of production and abatement is used where already known.

In operation, one of the necessities of this scheme of regulation (perhaps more so than with other schemes) is accurate source monitoring. In many cases, appropriate techniques of measurement do not exist. This is why we have earlier urged a greater research effort in the source monitoring field.

A third advantage of the economic-incentive approach is a gain in flexibility. A simple charge per unit of pollution is not the only form such a system can take, though it has the desirable feature of maintaining a constant incentive to reduce pollution. There are many variations. The law can mandate a relatively small charge for emissions up to a certain limit, and a stiff charge for exceeding that limit. The regulated industry is then not much penalized for minor excesses, but it is severely discouraged from going too far. As another alternative, monetary penalties can be charged for noncompliance with mandatory standards, as is now the case in Connecticut. This has the advantage of avoiding unrealistic penalties and time-consuming litigation. Regulatory charges can be varied relatively easily over time and space, or even for equity purposes.

There is, however, an important class of situations in which the minimum standard strategy is clearly superior, i.e., the case of a highly toxic material. Society wants to insure that the ambient concentration is safe, and the way to do that is to legislate it. Even if a sufficiently stiff regulatory charge could accomplish the same result, there is no good reason to accept the risk that the initial level of the charge might be too low, or that some change in costs might make the existing charge an insufficient deterrent.

Protection against toxic substances is an extreme case, but it points the way to the general answer. Where the primary objective is to achieve a given level of control with great certainty, and control cost is a minor matter, the standard-setting strategy is most appropriate. Where it is more important to get a grip on control costs, and fluctuations in the level of control achieved are a less important concern, the charge strategy would work most effectively. In the range of cases in between, one of the combined strategies, making use of both minimum standards and effluent charges, will usually prove to be the best.

At present, the legislation makes no provision even for experimentation with effluent-charge strategies. Several of our study committees concluded that such experimentation should be encouraged (see *Decision Making*, Chapter 6; *Research*, Chapter 2). The Noise Committee urges one or more carefully designed and monitored experiments confined to limited geographical areas and specific industries. Evaluation of such experiments could provide valuable information on effectiveness of regulatory charges. If necessary, explicit Congressional action should be sought both to authorize projects and to provide compensation, if necessary, for those who must bear the experimental costs incurred.

The Committee on Energy and the Environment concluded that the emission-charge strategy (or a related technique of auctioning off a budget of emission rights) may be a useful technique for preventing the deterioration of air quality in regions that are now cleaner than the national standards require (see *Energy*, Chapters 3 and 4). The Committee emphasized as still another important advantage of this strategy the creation of continuous pressure for technological innovation. The current system creates instead an incentive to generate arguments that prevention and abatement are impossible or prohibitively costly.

4 Next Steps

The National Research Council studies have given rise to many recommendations for action, some broad and some quite detailed. They are discussed and justified in the component reports. We hope they will be evaluated and elaborated by competent authorities in Congress, EPA, and other Executive agencies, and by environmentalists, affected industries, and the scientific community.

In setting forth the observations and judgments of those who guided the National Research Council program, this report has emphasized the major common themes. In conclusion, we can point to some steps that could be taken almost immediately, by EPA and by Congress, with clear advantage.

EPA could begin, as a matter of course, to do more explicit analysis and publish the results before making regulatory decisions. This would involve an assessment of the consequences of alternative courses of action—including no action—and an explicit statement of the uncertainties present and the value judgments invoked in the choice of a particular regulatory order. We believe that a conscientious attempt to follow this recommendation would dramatize the need for a greater investment in gathering, analyzing, and interpreting scientific and technical information for use in the decision-making process.

Another consequence of the attempt to do explicit analysis would be the need to develop much greater participation by outside scientists, engineers, economists, and others in the Agency's programs. We believe this would be good for EPA and for environmental policy. EPA could begin now to build the required bridges; their maintenance in the long run would require additional funds.

As part of the effort just described, the Science Advisory Board could be strengthened and made the primary institutional channel for communication with the scientific community at large. The Board should continue to serve the Administrator directly. Each research laboratory should establish advisory mechanisms to tap the knowledge and judgment of the outside scientific community.

Since the nature of environmental legislation has been part of the problem as well as part of the solution, some of our recommendations are addressed to Congress and especially the relevant committees.

Congress should rethink the laws themselves, especially (a) the extent to which their fragmented character has actually hindered the development of appropriate and effective policy; and (b) the possibility of encouraging experimentation with market incentives as a supplement to traditional regulatory standards, perhaps within the present statutory framework, perhaps after some amendment.

The success or failure of past decisions is also worth analyzing, not in a critical spirit of second guessing, but because much can be learned about improving decision making. Investigative studies of management and funding accountability by the Government Accounting Office should be helpful to EPA in this regard. But the Agency itself should commission continuous retrospective analyses of past decisions, so that internally generated information can be the basis for changes in procedures and processes.

A topic not covered in these studies is the detailed content of the current EPA research and development program. A number of the studies draw attention to research priorities and areas where opportunities for scientific investigation to assist the Agency are apparent (see *Monitoring* throughout); but, except in general terms (see *Research*, Chapters 2 and 3), no attempt was made to evaluate current allocations of funds or to suggest alternative research and development plans. Such continuous, detailed analysis must ultimately be the responsibility of the Agency, although the scientific and engineering communities can and should participate by serving on advisory panels, responding to requests for proposals, and submitting unsolicited proposals.

References

Kneese, A.V. and C.L. Schultze (1975) Pollution, Prices, and Public Policy. Washington, D.C.: The Brookings Institution.

National Commission on Water Quality (1976) Report to the Congress by the National Commission on Water Quality. Washington, D.C.: U.S. Government Printing Office.

National Research Council (1974a) Air Quality and Automobile Emission Control. Volume 1: Summary Report. A Report by the Coordinating Committee on Air Quality Studies, Commission on Natural Resources, National Research Council, National Academy of Sciences, National Academy of Engineering, for the Committee on Public Works, U.S. Congress, Senate. Committee Serial No. 93-24, 93rd Congress, 2nd Session.

National Research Council (1974b) Air Quality and Automobile Emission Control. Volume 2: Health Effects of Air Pollutants. A Report by the Coordinating Committee on Air Quality Studies, Commission on Natural Resources, National Research Council, National Academy of Sciences, National Academy of Engineering, for the Committee on Public Works, U.S. Congress, Senate. Committee Serial No. 93-24, 93rd Congress, 2nd Session.

National Research Council (1974c) Air Quality and Automobile Emission Control. Volume 3: The Relationship of Emissions to Ambient Air Quality. A Report by the Coordinating Committee on Air Quality Studies, Commission on Natural Resources, National Research Council, National Academy of Sciences, National Academy of Engineering, for the Committee on Public Works, U.S. Congress, Senate. Committee Serial No. 93-24, 93rd Congress, 2nd Session.

National Research Council (1974d) Air Quality and Automobile Emission Control. Volume 4: The Costs and Benefits of Automobile Emission Control. A Report by the Coordinating Committee on Air Quality Studies, Commission on Natural Resources, National Research Council, National Academy of Sciences, National Academy of Engineering, for the Committee on Public Works, U.S. Congress, Senate. Committee Serial No. 93-24, 93rd Congress, 2nd Session.

National Research Council (1975a) Air Quality and Stationary Source Emission Control. A Report by the Commission on Natural Resources, National Research Council, National Academy of Sciences, National Academy of Engineering, for the Committee on Public Works, U.S. Congress, Senate. Committee Serial No. 94-4, 94th Congress, 1st Session.

National Research Council (1975b) Decision Making for Regulating Chemicals in the Environment. A Report Prepared by the Commission on Natural Resources. Washington, D.C.: National Academy of Sciences.

National Research Council (1975c) Report of the Conference on Air Quality and Automobile Emissions. Committee on Environmental Decision Making, May 5. Washington, D.C.: National Academy of Sciences.

National Research Council (1976) Disposal in the Marine Environment—An Oceanographic Assessment. An Analytical Study for the U.S. Environmental Protection Agency. Washington, D.C.: National Academy of Sciences.

II SUMMARIES AND RECOMMENDATIONS

Specific Recommendations from the Report of the Committee on Environmental Decision Making

This report presents a number of recommendations for enhancing the use and acquisition of scientific and technical information in EPA decision making and for improving the Agency's decision-making processes and procedures. In developing these recommendations, the Committee paid particular attention to three aspects of decision making: the need for explicitness and analytical treatment of the consequences of a range of alternative EPA actions, the need for openness and access, and the importance and value of taking into account considerations of implementation of EPA decisions.

A. ANALYSIS IN SUPPORT OF DECISION MAKING

Although EPA's elaborate procedures for developing standards and regulations have significantly improved the quality of analysis by assuring open review of proposed actions, the analysis nevertheless often treats important factors inadequately. In its current decision-making processes, the Agency does not consistently include a systematic and comprehensive consideration of feasible alternatives.

● *EPA's decisions on standards and regulations should be supported by analyses that explicitly state the objectives of the decisions, identify feasible alternatives, evaluate (quantitatively, to the extent possible) the consequences of each alternative decision, explore potential problems in implementation, and indicate and examine the degree of uncertainty about the effects of EPA actions. The analyses should be available to the public.*

Systematic and well documented analyses could substantially improve the quality of EPA decisions by providing a framework for discussion and for public understanding of the factors that enter the decision process. The analyses would make possible the generation and evaluation of a more complete set of regulatory alternatives. Routine consideration of potential problems of implementing regulations and standards would help assure the practicality of EPA decisions. The careful consideration of uncertainties in available information and in the analyses would be useful both in directing the Agency's research efforts toward the resolution of those problems that appear to be particularly critical for decisions and in enhancing the credibility of EPA decisions. Even where existing legislation limits EPA's freedom to choose alternatives or consider certain factors, the Agency should assume responsibility for examining the consequences of various courses of action and making the analytic results available to the public. (For the full discussion supporting this recommendation see the corresponding Section A in the Committee's report.)

B. BARRIERS TO THE IMPLEMENTATION OF EPA REGULATIONS

Many EPA regulations are implemented by heterogeneous and relatively autonomous federal, state, and local government entities that have limited resources and varied incentives and constraints. Current EPA decision-making practices entail inadequate efforts to routinely consider the practicality of implementation by these different government entities. The failure to account for barriers to implementation can result in effects different from those intended when a regulation is published.

● *EPA should systematically take account of the difficulties of translating its rules into environmental action at the local level. The assessment of resource constraints and of other qualitative barriers to implementation should be an important concern in the formulation of new EPA regulations.*

For regulatory policies that entail activity by authorities outside headquarters, EPA should determine whether the full range of federal, state, and local government resources required for implementation are available, and when they are not, the Agency should either adopt an alternative policy with more realistic resource requirements or redeploy resources to meet anticipated needs or both. EPA can use program grants to states and localities for this purpose.

Those responsible for developing new regulations should also assess other qualitative impediments to implementation by states and localities. To help assure sensitivity to these practical considerations EPA should routinely prepare a summary declaration of implementation prospects for new regulations, covering such factors as conflicting organizational interests, lack of adequate information on performance by dischargers, and inappropriate incentives and disincentives for regulated entities, and the Agency should make this analysis available for critical review and comment by field authorities. (For the full discussion supporting this recommendation see the corresponding Section B in the Committee's report.)

C. ADVICE AND REVIEW FROM SCIENTISTS AND ENGINEERS OUTSIDE EPA

EPA often relies on previously unpublished or unreviewed data; this places a special burden on the Agency to make certain that the scientific and technical basis for its decisions is accurate and reliable. In addition, EPA does not have a regular and effective channel for advice to the Administrator from outside scientists and engineers, with the result that independent scientific judgments have not always been provided to the Administrator.

● *Scientific and technical data and analyses used in decision making should be reviewed routinely at an early stage to assure that all relevant data are considered and to reduce the possibility of misinterpretation or misuse of scientific results. In this process EPA will be greatly aided by the wide range of scientific and engineering expertise that exists outside the Agency. The reviews should be available to the public as a matter of course.*

● *On decisions that set significant precedents or have a substantial impact on public health or welfare or on public or private expenditures, the Administrator personally should have access to independent scientific advice and evaluations of the overall technical basis for decisions.*

This can best be accomplished by increasing the responsibilities of the existing Science Advisory Board (SAB) so that its chairman would serve full time for a fixed term and would convey independent evaluations of scientific and technical data and analyses directly to the Administrator. In addition, the Chairman of the SAB should have explicit authority to initiate SAB activity on issues for which he or she judges scientific and technical advice to be warranted. (For the full discussion supporting this recommendation see the corresponding Section C in the Committee's report.)

D. DEPENDENCE ON REGULATED INDUSTRIES FOR DATA AND ANALYSIS

EPA is inevitably dependent on the industries it regulates for much of the technical and economic information it uses in decision making. The impact of many decisions on industry creates a potential conflict of interest that may cause industry either inadvertently or intentionally to distort or withhold necessary information. EPA is particularly dependent on industrial data for: (1) the determination of the toxic effects of substances released to the environment; and (2) the assessment of the costs and technical feasibility of pollution control devices and of engineering alternatives in production processes to achieve pollution control.

● *EPA should develop sufficient scientific and technical expertise within the Agency or through independent institutions and should institute procedures to assure the quality, reliability, relevance, and completeness of data provided by industry for EPA's use.*

EPA should extend its development and publication of guidelines and protocols to apply to all toxicological testing and should insure their use. This is particularly important now that legislation to control commercially available toxic substances has been enacted. In addition, laboratories performing toxicological tests should be certified as having acceptable facilities, personnel, and standards of performance, and EPA should eventually accept data only from certified laboratories. A program of "spot checks" of certified laboratories, and selective audits of reported results, should be undertaken to monitor the maintenance of standards for toxicological testing.

To minimize its dependence on industry for information on pollution control technology or industrial processes, EPA should use and support those few independent experts in this area currently in government laboratories, universities, and research organizations. Where independent expertise in areas central to EPA's interests and responsibilities does not exist, the Agency should develop technical programs consisting primarily of research and development activities within EPA, in other governmental laboratories, or in independent institutions so that appropriate expertise can be developed and maintained. (For the full discussion supporting this recommendation see the corresponding Section D in the Committee's report.)

E. SCIENTIFIC AND TECHNICAL RESEARCH IN SUPPORT OF DECISION MAKING

EPA's research and development programs alone are not adequate to serve either its current requirements for technical data and analyses or its long-term need to expand knowledge of the physical, biological, economic, and social phenomena related to problems of environmental regulation.

● *The principal role of EPA's in-house laboratories should be to perform research and supply technical expertise responsive to immediate Agency needs. These laboratories should be assessed for the quality and relevance of their work and their efforts redirected where necessary. The exchange of information and views between the research and development activities and the regulatory activities of the Agency should be improved, and the scientific leaders in EPA should be more deeply involved in the regulatory decision-making process.*

● *In those technical areas in which in-house capability is neither adequate nor feasible to develop (given the realities of political and bureaucratic constraints), EPA should use research centers outside the Agency; research that can better be done in other existing governmental laboratories, such as certain studies of health effects, should be carried out in those laboratories and supported by EPA.*

● *EPA should support a strong, stable, long-term program in environmental research in areas central to its regulatory responsibilities.*

Such research is best performed in institutions insulated from the inevitable day-to-day pressures of a regulatory agency. In addition to providing needed information, such a long-term program would assure development of a base of scientific and technical expertise and of facilities for training scientists and engineers who could eventually serve the federal government, state governments, industry, local communities, and public interest groups. (For the full discussion supporting this recommendation see the corresponding Section E in the Committee's report.)

F. STATUTORY DEADLINES ON ADMINISTRATIVE ACTIONS

At times, statutory deadlines on EPA administrative actions have had the disadvantage of forcing the Agency to make decisions without the benefit of new, potentially useful information; but, on balance, they have had a beneficial effect on the Agency's decision making. The major disadvantage of deadlines could be removed if statutes were to permit extensions in cases in which additional information, essential to sound decision making, would be available in a reasonable amount of time.

● *Statutory deadlines should continue to be imposed on EPA's administrative actions. They should reflect a realistic view of the time required to make a reasonable assessment of available information. There should be provisions permitting EPA to extend deadlines under certain conditions and for specified periods.*

Any authority granted EPA to use extension provisions should be conditional on the Agency establishing that: (a) it requires additional time to gather or interpret technical information identified by EPA as essential to a decision; (b) it has made an effort in good faith to obtain this information; and (c) it has considered the adverse effects of postponement. When EPA has decided on the need for and duration of an extension, it should issue a public notice well in advance of the original deadline. EPA's decision should be subject to review by a federal Court of Appeals at the time of the public notice.

In the case of deadlines for submission of comment by interested parties on EPA's proposed rule making, there is a need to provide more time for better informed and more effective comment. (For the full discussion supporting this recommendation see the corresponding Section F in the Committee's report.)

G. PROCEDURAL REQUIREMENTS FOR DECISION MAKING

Traditional procedural requirements established by statutes and court decisions for agency action have not always been well suited to the types of decisions made by EPA. As a result, EPA, under the direction of federal courts and on its own initiative, has experimented with innovations in procedures. A number of these innovations have had a beneficial effect on the decision-making process and can be used more widely. Several additional changes in the procedures could be developed to assist in decision making and to make the decision-making process more open to external review.

● *EPA should make greater use of procedural innovations developed within EPA and other federal agencies that, when combined with steps to increase openness in the Agency and the use of explicit analysis, will reduce the need to rely on formal procedures characteristic of trials and adjudications.*

Unless formal trial procedures are required by law, EPA should use procedures that may be less time consuming and expensive than trial-type procedures, such as the exchange of documents and informal questioning. Such procedures should neither materially reduce the consideration of scientific and technical information, nor deny parties fairness or due process of law.

Formal trial procedures generally should not be imposed on EPA decision-making processes; however, when Congress has chosen to do so, steps should be taken to streamline the procedures.

EPA should institute a more orderly procedure for compiling the relevant documentary record and making its contents easily available to the public. In addition, EPA should explicitly define and adhere to policies stating which information submitted by regulated parties and which internal memoranda should be available to the public.

EPA should make public an understandable summary of the rationale for each regulatory decision (including decisions not to take action) by publishing at the time of notice of proposed rule making a complete statement of the basis for its findings and its reasoning, including descriptions of (1) the scientific, economic, and other information (including information on statutory requirements and judicial decisions) relied on to evaluate the alternatives and the uncertainties in the information; (2) the analyses used in making the decision; and (3) the relative importance given to conflicting considerations in reaching the decision. Revisions of this statement should be included within the preamble to the final decision. (For the full discussion supporting this recommendation see the corresponding Section G in the Committee's report.)

H. INTERAGENCY REVIEW

The requirement that proposed and final EPA regulations be circulated for formal review to other federal agencies and the Office of Management and Budget (OMB) prior to publication has had a positive effect on the

Agency's decisions. Environmentalists have expressed concern that the reviews may lead to undue influence by those who emphasize national goals that conflict with environmental improvement. Although experience in a few cases has supported this concern, it is overshadowed by the improved EPA analysis of the consequences of its actions that has resulted, at least in part, from the review process. Interagency review can, however, unnecessarily delay the promulgation of EPA rules.

● *For proposed rules, present procedures for interagency review should be retained, except that they should be conducted concurrently with public notice-and-comment procedures rather than preceding them. Interagency review of final regulations should be greatly expedited. Some of the time saved by these changes should be used to extend the period for outside comments on proposed rules and to introduce a short period for submission of replies to the first round of comments.*

The prescribed procedural change would allow extension of the review-and-comment period both for the interested executive agencies and for private parties without lengthening the total duration of the decision process. (For the full discussion supporting this recommendation see the corresponding Section H in the Committee's report.)

I. JUDICIAL REVIEW

Judicial review of EPA's administrative actions has played a major role in shaping and improving the Agency's decision-making process. The judicial review process has impeded EPA's programs only when federal courts have given conflicting interpretations to statutes intended to be administered uniformly throughout the country.

● *The current structure and standards for judicial review should be maintained with the exception that legislative changes should be made to provide that certain EPA decisions that apply uniformly over the nation be reviewed only in the U.S. Court of Appeals for the District of Columbia.*
(For the full discussion supporting this recommendation see the corresponding Section I in the Committee's report.)

J. PUBLIC PARTICIPATION

Citizen organizations have played a significant role in EPA's development and implementation of environmental policy. However, the extent of their involvement is limited by the amount of funds available for public participation in EPA and judicial proceedings.

● *EPA, perhaps through an impartial body, should provide some of the financial support of groups or individuals who can contribute to rule making or adjudicatory proceedings by raising new issues or by submitting additional assessments or analyses of relevant issues. To gain an understanding of difficulties of implementation, the Agency should experiment with means for providing such support.*

Determination of eligibility and amount of award should be based upon an applicant's demonstration of potential contribution to the proceedings (that would not otherwise be made by other participants) and of financial need. EPA should allocate a fixed sum for a public participation program that reflects the general experience with contributions of citizen groups.

In addition to this program of participation in administrative proceedings before EPA, court fee awards should be extended to all types of environmental litigation by statutory change where necessary. Existing statutory citizen suit provisions should be expanded by enacting for each EPA statute a uniform provision to deal with all aspects of suits initiated by citizens.

EPA's current means of awarding grants and contracts should be used to a greater extent to solicit or sponsor citizen group research and public education relevant to regulatory issues. (For the full discussion supporting this recommendation see the corresponding section J in the Committee's report.)

K. PRIORITIES

The establishment of priorities for EPA programs has been heavily influenced by factors beyond the Agency's control. At least until recently the most significant external factor was the detailed legislative direction written into the major environmental statutes. However, within the statutory requirements EPA has a great deal of discretion in establishing its priorities. The Agency is now entering a period in which most of the action-forcing deadlines in the statutes have passed and the laws' mandates are thus no longer as significant in establishing Agency priorities as they were. Continued responsiveness to external forces is appropriate, providing internal safeguards are set up against unproductive uses of Agency resources. Current Agency procedures for setting priorities do not assure that, within the discretion allowed by Congress,

EPA resources are routinely assigned where there is greatest need and opportunity for environmental protection.

● *EPA's priorities should be established more explicitly, openly, and systematically to achieve the greatest expected improvement in environmental quality with available pollution control resources; ideally, the estimation of expected improvement in environmental quality should be based on quantitative measures of environmental conditions.*

Several improvements are required. (1) For each EPA program area, decisions about which pollution problems the program will address, and the long-term control strategy for each, should culminate in a regularly updated strategy document that is analytic in character. This document should lay out the current scientific basis for the chosen strategy and should include attempts to estimate the expected environmental improvement. (2) The Agency should better integrate the various components of its present priority-setting procedures; in particular, short-term priorities and decisions about annual resource allocations within the Agency should be based on a logical relationship to stated longer-term program goals and strategies. (3) Documents supporting the establishment of priorities should make clear what assumptions are used to relate proposed actions to anticipated environmental consequences, and the uncertainties inherent in these assumptions should be used as indicators of the Agency's research needs. (4) Drafts of priority documents should be available for outside review both as a check on EPA's facts and analyses and to facilitate communication of EPA program goals both within and outside the Agency. Suitable modification of current EPA procedures can provide the necessary improvement without burdensome administrative cost. (For the full discussion supporting this recommendation see the corresponding Section K in the Committee's report.)

L. ORGANIZATIONAL FEEDBACK

EPA has not adequately developed or used information on the effectiveness of its past decisions. Agency data management practices make it difficult to identify long-term trends in environmental quality, and monitoring systems provide little information that is useful in the formulation of specific regulations or the evaluation of EPA programs. In addition, there is too little objective information available to headquarters decision makers on incentives and disincentives affecting the actions of local implementing authorities and individual dischargers. The Agency is missing opportunities to learn from its first five years of experience in making major regulatory decisions.

● *The Agency should initiate programs to assure feedback information on the implications of its actions in three areas.*

Environmental indicators: To better assess the ultimate environmental impacts of its actions, EPA should improve its use of monitoring data in decision making and should develop management-oriented environmental indicators that can be used to gauge environmental progress.

The Agency should improve its collection and, more particularly, its analysis of environmental data so that it has a usable, reliable, and timely set of measures of environmental conditions. A set of reliable environmental indicators should be selected and used to enhance EPA's ability to evaluate past program effectiveness on a regular basis, to help set program priorities, and to facilitate analysis of policy alternatives for new regulations. Summary data should be reported to the public on a regular and consistent basis so that long-term environmental trends can be identified and appreciated.

Implementation studies: To improve its understanding of the pragmatic problems of applying regulations to individual dischargers, EPA should initiate a regular program of implementation studies. As part of the program, EPA should reexamine the effectiveness of its formal reporting system and its practices for awarding program grants to state and local governments.

EPA should establish a continuing program of special studies to generate and evaluate information on the outcomes of past regulatory actions. These implementation studies should examine factors that affect the actual application of these regulations to dischargers, and should assess any discrepancies between intended and observed outcomes. The results of these studies will help the Agency to assess the relative merits of the various administrative approaches that have been tried by different regional offices, states, and localities.

Retrospective analysis: To improve analyses supporting regulatory decisions, the Agency should initiate a series of retrospective reviews of the adequacy of past analyses.

A somewhat smaller study effort should be devoted to reviews of the quality and adequacy of policy analyses for a sample of past EPA regulations. These reviews would elucidate the relative value of alternative information-handling procedures, provide insights into the accuracy of data sources, and reveal "blind spots" (for instance, faulty assumptions about the ease of implementing a regulation) and their causes. (For the full discussion supporting this recommendation see the corresponding Section L in the Committee's report.)

M. MORE EFFECTIVE SANCTIONS

Speed and flexibility of application and credibility are important qualities of the sanctions that can be applied for violations of environmental regulations. Among possible types of sanctions, civil penalties that can be imposed by administrative action are particularly notable for these qualities; however, a number of statutes administered by EPA do not explicitly provide the Agency with civil penalty authority. In addition, existing "all or nothing" financial sanctions against state and local governments not in compliance with EPA grant requirements fail to provide the necessary flexibility and credibility to be effective.

● *EPA should vigorously use its authority to assess civil penalties without going to court. Where such authority has not yet been conferred, statutes should be amended to increase the availability and utility of such sanctions.*

The authority to assess civil penalties by administrative rather than judicial action should include the use of (a) penalties to deter one time or noncontinuous violations (such as the misuse of a pesticide, the failure to report emission data to EPA, or the unlawful spill of a pollutant), and (b) noncompliance fees to encourage the quick adoption of abatement measures by sources emitting pollution in excess of EPA standards.

● *EPA should modify its sanctions under grant requirements to provide for the use of less severe penalties than withdrawal of the grant. The Agency should also develop alternative sanctions that would create incentives for the states to implement environmental regulations effectively.*

(For the full discussion supporting this recommendation see the corresponding Section M in the Committee's report.)

N. ALTERNATIVE STRATEGIES

The current regulatory mode used for pollution control does not provide for significant attention to cost-effectiveness nor does it provide for the use of economic incentives, including effluent charges. Operating entirely within the regulatory mode, the Agency has opportunities for improved cost effectiveness in achieving environmental objectives. The opportunities could be realized, in some cases, without alteration of the current legislative framework; in other cases, statutory constraints would have to be changed. Effluent charges, used either in conjunction with or as a substitute for regulation, have some theoretical advantages and may enable EPA to achieve the goals of environmental protection with greater cost effectiveness.

● *The current regulatory framework used by EPA should be revised and supplemented to allow the use of management strategies that may be more cost-effective in achieving environmental objectives and that experiment with greater use of economic incentives, including effluent charges.*

The potential costs associated with constraints on cost-effective means of achieving environmental objectives, such as some statutory requirements of uniformity, should be examined. Where such costs are substantial they should be brought to the attention of Congress.

In general, the regulatory mode is preferable when there is an unwillingness to run the risk of not achieving some overriding environmental objective (such as the elimination of a highly toxic substance). The effluent charge strategy has most promise in those cases where lack of knowledge makes the optimal level of ambient standards uncertain, and where the aim is to achieve significant improvements in the environment with minimal adverse impact on the economy. (For the full discussion supporting this recommendation see the corresponding section N in the Committee's report.)

O. EPA'S ROLE UNDER THE NATIONAL ENVIRONMENTAL POLICY ACT

EPA has a statutory obligation to act as an environmental advocate within the federal government through its review of the environmental impact statements of other federal agencies. EPA review should be superior to private litigation as a prompt and informed means for assessing impact statement adequacy, and for this reason EPA should carry out its review more vigorously.

● *EPA should devote more resources, including sufficient technical staff support, to the discharge of its review function. The Agency should comment at the earliest possible opportunity on expected adverse impacts caused or condoned by the actions of other agencies, emphasizing impacts likely to involve the exercise of EPA regulatory authority at a later date.*

(For the full discussion supporting this recommendation see the corresponding Section O in the Committee's report.)

Summary from the Report of the Environmental Research Assessment Committee

In discharging its regulatory responsibilities, EPA must make decisions that require sound scientific support. The purpose of this report is to suggest how the Agency might organize and use research to meet these needs for critical information.

Consideration of the complexities of regulatory decision making for environmental protection and of the legislative directives and constraints under which the Agency must work has convinced the Environmental Research Assessment Committee (1) that it is both appropriate and necessary for EPA to continue to perform and sponsor research, and (2) that the primary purposes of the Agency's research program should be to provide technical support to the decision-making process and to anticipate future environmental problems.

These two conclusions, and recognition that the Agency performs its regulatory functions in an adversary legal system, are basic to the argument of this report. In this framework the Committee formulated its conclusions and recommendations.

This report examines: the need for research (see Chapter 1); the components of an effective research program, and where and how they should be carried out (see Chapter 2); and the organization and management of this program, from planning to transfer of results (see Chapters 3, 4, and 5).

The major recommendations are summarized below. Some of them address important policy issues: the need for a coordinated federal environmental research and development program; the role of EPA's

Office of Research and Development in providing support for the Agency's decision-making process; and the scope of EPA's research mandate. Other recommendations in the report, some of which are highlighted in this summary, are intended to improve both the effectiveness and the credibility of the Agency's research and development program.

MAJOR RECOMMENDATIONS

THE ROLE OF RESEARCH IN EPA

● *EPA's research and development should concentrate primarily on support of the Agency's decision making and anticipation of future problems.*

● *EPA should supplement its primary research responsibilities with some fundamental research to help advance understanding in environmental sciences and technology.*

● *A new legislative mandate will be required if EPA is to conduct effective anticipatory and fundamental research.*

For an agency whose principal mission is regulation, and whose funds for research are necessarily limited, the emphasis of its scientific and technical activities must be support of the regulatory function. At present, the legislative mandates for EPA's research come from the individual programs of ten major laws. While this situation is appropriate and necessary for providing support for decision making in these programs, there is also a need for research that goes beyond this immediate support. The Agency has been restrained from conducting or supporting the research of longer range and wider scope needed to anticipate problems and to advance understanding by having its research authorities associated only with specific programs for environmental protection. EPA should not, however, be considered a lead agency in fundamental research on environmental science and technology. (For full discussion see the sections in Chapter 1 on Purposes of Environmental Research and Assessing the Role of EPA in Environmental Research and in Chapter 2 on Investigation of Fundamental Physical, Chemical, and Biological Processes.)

THE NEED FOR A COORDINATED FEDERAL ENVIRONMENTAL
RESEARCH AND DEVELOPMENT PROGRAM

● *We recommend that the Office of Science and Technology Policy (OSTP) develop a federal environmental research, development, and demonstration strategy that includes designation of the appropriate roles of all participating federal agencies and existing interagency coordinating committees, and delineation of the relationships between federal and nonfederal research and development. The OSTP should coordinate the implementation of the strategy through its mandated consultations with the Office of Management and Budget (OMB) about the scientific programs of federal agencies.*

If protecting the environment is to be accorded a status commensurate with the impacts of environmental problems on national domestic affairs, more of the national research and development effort must be devoted to these problems than can or should be deployed by EPA alone. To provide information needed for sound environmental decision making, the federal environmental research and development program must be more effectively planned and coordinated than it is at present. Because the potential partners in the needed cooperative effort are located at several levels of administration in the federal bureaucracy, and because the budgetary process is the most effective tool for implementing a coordinated research plan, responsibility for overview and coordination should lie in the Executive Office of the President. The recommendation specifies OSTP because of its mandates to assist the President in providing leadership and coordination of federal research and development programs and to consult with the OMB on the scientific programs of federal agencies. (See the section in Chapter 1 on Coordination of Research Programs.)

ORGANIZATION OF EPA'S RESEARCH

● *We recommend that the management of all research and development in EPA be centralized in the Office of Research and Development (OR&D).*

There are advantages and disadvantages, detailed in Chapter 3, to centralizing responsibility for the Agency's research and development activities in OR&D. On balance, the advantages, such as encouragement of research whose concerns are not limited by artificial boundaries in the environment often prescribed by legislation, outweigh the disadvantages. Further, some of the disadvantages can be overcome by good management practices, some of which are detailed in Chapters 4 and 5. (An example is the use of personnel from Program Offices on detail to OR&D to act as project managers for extramural research.) The recommendation applies to all the Agency's ongoing, substantial research and development, but not to routine laboratory and technical services now being performed in Program and Regional Offices.

● *EPA's research program needs to be better organized for balance and continuity, through planning developed around a logical conceptual framework of environmental protection (such as we propose in Chapters 1 and 2).*

More attention should be given to systematic assessment of existing information for decision makers, analysis of environmental trends, integration of studies of impacts in different media, and socioeconomic research. The Agency should continue its recent efforts to plan research farther ahead so that more research can be done in anticipation of decisions, rather than in response to crises.

● *A central function of scientific support to decision making should be to provide integrated assessments of available scientific, technical, and economic data pertinent to pending decisions in forms suitable for use by Agency decision makers. We recommend that the importance of this function be recognized by giving it formal status and organization in OR&D.*

Integrated analysis of available data transfers technical information from the research community to decision makers, a service vital to the decision-making process. At present this function is being performed on an ad hoc basis with personnel "borrowed" from other activities. (For a description of this function, see Chapter 2 on Assessment and Integration of Available Information, and Chapter 5 on Applications of the Results of R&D. For detailed suggestions on the organization of the proposed office, see Chapter 3 on Consequences for OR&D's Program.)

● *The research planning system now in use in OR&D, characterized as "top-down" in structure, should be retained for research in support of decision making. For anticipatory and fundamental research, however, we recommend a "bottom-up" scheme that relies on the scientific community to identify research needs.*

Research in support of decision making should respond to needs identified by the potential users, decision makers in EPA, entailing a "top-down" scheme. The scientific and technical communities, both inside and outside EPA, are best qualified to identify needs for anticipatory and fundamental research, entailing a "bottom-up" scheme. (Both are described and illustrated in the section in Chapter 4 on Identifying Research Needs.)

● *We recommend that block funding of extramural grants, contracts, and interagency agreements be considered as a mechanism to establish centers of excellence, federally funded contract research and development laboratories, and umbrella interagency agreements to supplement the intramural research and development program.*

The increased flexibility and continuity of the recommended funding arrangements will reduce the time required to initiate research. Block funding establishes and maintains extramural research capabilities that perform as extensions of the intramural program, and results in work more closely attuned to the Agency's programs and purposes than that performed by extramural researchers selected on an ad hoc basis (see Chapter 3 on The Extramural Program).

TECHNICAL QUALITY OF RESEARCH

● *All proposals and completed research should be subjected to review on their technical merits by scientific and technical peers.*

To judge scientific and technical merit, there is no substitute for review of proposals, progress, and results of both projects and programs by peers in the scientific and technical communities, both inside and outside EPA. Peer review of the scientific merit of proposals will assure that work plans are technically sound and determine whether the proposed research has already been conducted elsewhere (see Chapter 4 on Managing Scientific Activities for discussion of this and other recommendations for improving the technical quality and effectiveness of EPA research).

● *We recommend the use of a parallel grade advancement system, based on performance of research, that does not require researchers to assume administrative or managerial tasks to attain promotions.*

Improving working conditions in this way may be expected to help attract and keep the best research talent and consequently to improve the quality of research programs (see Chapter 4 on Personnel and Facilities for discussion of this and other recommendations for managing the Agency's research personnel).

Summary of the
Report of the
Study Group on
Environmental Monitoring

The Study Group on Environmental Monitoring has written the following summary of its report. Many recommendations to improve monitoring for environmental management are addressed to EPA; some are addressed to other agencies and to industry. The more important recommendations are italicized.

MAJOR CONCLUSIONS

When it was created, EPA was challenged to direct and guide environmental programs while confronted with large gaps in scientific knowledge, constrained by excessively detailed specifications in legislation, and hampered by its own fragmented formation and inheritance. The Agency had to establish its programs at great speed. Certain directions it had to take were obvious, and the development of integrated and efficient scientific monitoring programs could not receive priority. Now, however, information from monitoring is essential to the formulation, implementation, and evaluation of environmental management policies to protect human health and well-being at acceptable cost. EPA should take a comprehensive look at monitoring and work toward improvement of its own monitoring programs and those that support its mission in other agencies. The Study Group on Environmental Monitoring finds EPA's current monitoring programs seriously deficient in three major ways.

INADEQUATE USE OF SCIENTIFIC PRINCIPLES

First, EPA does not adequately apply scientific principles to the design, operation, and evaluation of monitoring programs. Programs are too often developed hastily in response to the dictates of legislation and enforcement procedures and the exigencies of pollution control management, instead of being based on clear objectives, priorities, and criteria related to a national montoring system. As a result, current monitoring does not adequately serve the important purposes of evaluating the progress of national environmental programs in terms of changes in environmental quality and of determining relationships among sources of pollution, ambient environmental quality, and effects on humans, animals, and plants.

NEED TO MONITOR FOR ANTICIPATION AND DISCOVERY

Second, EPA's almost exclusive emphasis on monitoring to control sources of pollution, rather than to discover and anticipate environmental problems, meets only short-term goals. EPA needs to take care of the environment over the longer term, and this responsibility involves more than controlling effluents. It involves, at the least, detecting new environmental problems in early stages, and, at best, anticipating them before they occur. Monitoring programs must be designed to help in understanding causes of pollution, to measure trends in levels of residuals, and to keep watch on the responses of humans, animals, and plants to changes in environmental quality. Without monitoring programs designed for these purposes, the nation is too frequently surprised by environmental crises, and it responds hastily with special studies and hurried legislation, regulations, and enforcement programs. These responses result in monitoring and control policies that are less efficient than they could be.

FRAGMENTATION OF MONITORING

Third, responsibilities for monitoring are fragmented. There is inadequate coordination of monitoring among local, state, regional, and federal agencies, and even among EPA programs themselves. Separate programs often exist where a single program could serve multiple needs; pollutants are measured in one medium that are not measured in others; data on water pollution are collected that are not accompanied by data on flow; and the synthesis of pollution data and the study of relationships between pollution and its effects are hindered by incompatible data collection and processing methods. And because knowledge from disparate scientific disciplines relevant to monitoring is not sufficiently integrated, many types of scientific expertise are absent from the design and evaluation of monitoring systems. The result is that monitoring programs are designed and operated with little or no assessment of their contribution to a national monitoring system or to the success of an overall national environmental program.

RECOMMENDATIONS

SCIENTIFIC LEADERSHIP

Along with significant gaps in environmental monitoring, there is a proliferation of uncoordinated, inefficient, and inflexible monitoring programs that produce data of poor or unknown quality. We conclude that a basic reason for these problems is that environmental sciences in EPA lack leadership in positions that could influence monitoring. Particularly in sciences of environmental monitoring, scientific leadership in the Agency should be developed and given organizational support.

● *We recommend that, within the EPA Administrator's office, an Office of Science be established to exert scientific leadership in EPA, to aid its programs by better integration of scientific principles, and to improve data collection by more scientific influence and direction.* (See Chapter 4.)

If an Office of Science is not established, other means should be found to assure that scientific principles are applied to the design, operation, and evaluation of monitoring programs. From our examinations of a number of monitoring activities, we conclude that EPA's current management of monitoring does not accomplish these important objectives.

EPA's role in the design of ambient water quality monitoring networks is an example of inadequate application of scientific principles. EPA has proposed new networks to replace a current one without evident analysis of the existing network to justify the change. Valuable research is supported by the Agency, including research on monitoring network design, but rarely are the findings applied.

Most monitoring of ambient environmental quality is done by state and local agencies. It is neither necessary nor desirable for EPA to collect all data firsthand, but it is essential that the definition of objectives and the resolution of primary questions of monitoring network design, data management, quality assurance, and cost-effectiveness be the concerns of

EPA's central office. We propose that these responsibilities be among those assumed specifically by the Agency's Office of Science.

USE OF PROTOTYPES

Prior to establishing or changing either a data collection procedure of a national monitoring program or a data processing operation, EPA should develop and evaluate prototypes to insure that data will effectively meet specified needs.

• *We recommend that EPA, through its Office of Science, base its proposals and designs for ambient monitoring networks on prototype studies developed in cooperation with other federal agencies and the states.* (See Chapter 2.)

MANAGEMENT OF SCIENTIFIC DATA

Evaluation of Data Collection and Processing

Fragmentation of monitoring activities within EPA is most evident from the proliferation of separate and uncoordinated data processing and information handling systems (see Chapter 3). It is unclear how most of the data in these systems are related to EPA decision making.

• *We recommend that a review and evaluation be made for each current and proposed data processing or information handling system of the Agency in conjunction with its associated monitoring programs.* (See Chapter 3.) *This review requires that EPA answer the basic questions: Who are the beneficiaries of the data and the system, and what are the specific benefits? How do the data and the system contribute to environmental management, and what high priority needs of the Agency do they meet?*

This review demands work by a full-time professional group, not by part-time advisory groups alone. The review should be among the duties of the Office of Science.

Obtaining Better Measurements

The fledgling quality assurance activities of EPA are uncoordinated and inadequately funded. Those responsible have little authority to see that uniform definitions and protocols are used. More and broader national programs of interlaboratory comparisons are needed to determine the accuracy of data on environmental characteristics and to maintain accuracy and stimulate improvements. Until these deficiencies are corrected, most of the data on which policies ought to be based will be of poor or unknown accuracy.

● *We recommend that a continuing certification program be established for those laboratories that, by performing measurements, determine whether industries and state and local governments are complying with permits or standards.* (See Chapter 3.)

Such certification should be based on performance and not solely on evaluations of personnel, equipment, and methods.

Pollution control strategies are often developed from inventories based on an enumeration of sources and estimates of emissions from them. Thus, mistakes in these inventories can be costly. EPA should develop a source inventory quality assurance program to evaluate different methods for compiling inventories and to provide standard definitions of sources.

For each pollutant that EPA requires to be monitored, the Agency establishes a reference measurement method, an authorized protocol for sampling and measuring a level of concentration. As part of this procedure, EPA should study alternative measurement methods to determine their compatibility and to develop ways of relating the results of one method to those of another.

Data Analysis and Dissemination

If it is to make informed decisions, EPA should analyze the data it acquires. It appears, however, that most of these data are not analyzed adequately. Since data collection is expensive, EPA should determine that data not only meet their intended purposes efficiently but that they serve as many purposes as possible. The Agency should analyze its environmental data in relation to various purposes they could serve, such as evaluating national monitoring networks, measuring the progress of environmental programs, and studying relationships between pollution and its effects. In addition, EPA should summarize its data in more informative annual reports and disseminate data earlier and more widely to others who would find them helpful. EPA research reports, at least those that may have a major impact on public policy, should undergo external scientific review, and some should be submitted to refereed journals. The Agency should also publish the scientific and economic analyses upon which its decisions are based.

Statistical Resources in EPA

The problems with EPA's management of scientific data are exacerbated by the paucity of statistical talent in the Agency. In addition to producing and consuming data about the environment, EPA has many statistical responsibilities. For example, the Agency writes environmental guidelines and standards that must take account of natural variability, and it specifies statistical measures in regulations that must be designed for efficient enforcement. Statisticians are needed to cooperate with other scientists in improving the design of experiments and surveys and in improving techniques for sampling, data analyses, quality assurance, and decision making under uncertainty. EPA should develop, particularly in its Office of Science, sufficient talent to meet its many statistical responsibilities.

NEW PROGRAMS

Some of our recommendations are that organizations other than EPA develop and maintain data that would be used in support of EPA's mission. EPA itself should further these efforts by appropriate persuasion, financial sponsorship, or support of legislation.

Health Effects of Air Pollution

A long-term epidemiological study is needed to measure the health benefits of air pollution control. Many difficulties must be faced: the design of the study should consider the accuracy and relevance of measurements of both health and the environment, the high correlations among levels of many pollutants, and the effect of omitting pollutants that contribute to harmful effects. EPA should not be solely responsible for such a complex enterprise.

● *We recommend that careful planning begin immediately among various agencies most involved for a long-term, multi-city study of the effects of air pollution on human health, including both chronic and acute disease.* (See Chapter 2.)

For estimating the exposure of the population, the study should pay special attention to the use of personal monitors and mobile vans, along with models, to supplement fixed stations. We also recommend that EPA support the development of personal air pollution monitors and move toward further measuring and reporting the respirable fraction of particulate matter.

Monitoring to Anticipate Pollution Problems

We considered ways in which programs to monitor the components and expected wastes of industrial processes, the transportation of possibly hazardous substances, and the operation of wastewater treatment plants could provide information to anticipate pollution problems.

No programs currently require industry to monitor the components of its manufacturing processes even though, in many cases, industry is already capable of doing so. Such monitoring could detect changes from routine operations and thereby provide warning of unusual types of residuals or increased levels of familiar residuals so that their environmental effects could be anticipated and diminished. The practice should be fostered.

In addition, before a new product is manufactured or a new process instituted, industry should analyze the expected waste to identify the substances that will be discharged and to assess their potential effect on the environment. The information should be made available to EPA and state environmental protection agencies.

Current efforts by federal agencies to prevent transportation accidents that cause pollution are inadequate. Although EPA may regulate the transportation of hazardous wastes, no federal agency has the authority to require carriers to report their plans for transporting other possibly hazardous chemicals. Routine reporting is not needed, but rather the authority for an agency to monitor transport when and where it poses a danger to the public. In addition, EPA and carriers should formulate guidelines and plans for the safe transport of potentially hazardous substances. At the least, bills of lading for such substances should include the scientific name of chemicals being shipped.

In view of evidence that many municipal wastewater treatment plants are not operating as designed, EPA should provide better monitoring procedures and technical assistance for evaluating the efficiency of such plants and for determining whether problems are due to overloading, management, or design. EPA could thus improve the design and operation of treatment plants and determine whether, in achieving water quality standards, it is more efficient to allocate resources to municipal sewerage systems for operation and maintenance than for construction.

Monitoring to Discover Environmental Problems

We recommend a number of programs to improve EPA's ability to discover environmental problems early by keeping timely watch on changes in environmental quality and the responses of humans, animals, and plants (see Chapter 3). Determining changes requires the establishment of a base from which to measure.

Baseline Monitoring The discovery of the toxic effects of many chemicals leads to questions concerning their occurrence in the environment. Base levels for many of these chemicals could be established, ideally, with a quantitative assessment now of parts of the environment that could be scrutinized years later to detect the presence of chemicals that proved to have adverse effects. With modern techniques, such as gas chromatography and mass spectrometry, analytical records of selected samples can be preserved.

● *We recommend that EPA analyze samples of the environment for the presence and quantity of selected chemicals and preserve analytical records for retrospective analyses of other chemicals.*

Samples of air, water, soil, and biota should be periodically collected from various regions and analyzed. Gas chromatograms and mass spectrograms should be preserved for retrospective analyses of chemicals that subsequently are suspected to have adverse effects. (See Chapter 2.)

There is evidence that acidic precipitation has been increasing in some areas of the United States and that it has a number of deleterious effects. It may leach nutrients from the soil and impede the growth of vegetation; it may reduce the abundance and diversity of fish and micro-flora and fauna of rivers and lakes; and it may increase the corrosion of materials.

● *We recommend the establishment, following prototype studies, of a national network to monitor the acidity and other characteristics of precipitation and particulates that fall to earth.* (See Chapter 2.)

Surveillance of Humans A promising activity of monitoring for discovery is surveillance to detect changes in human mutation rates. Findings of no increase in mutation rates would provide reassurance. Findings of increased mutation rates would provide evidence for the regulation of man-made mutagens and might need to be followed by studies to determine causal agents. Monitoring genetic effects in humans is now technically feasible, but many important problems remain to be studied. We recommend that research policy conferences be sponsored to discuss the scientific, social, and cost–benefit problems of monitoring for genetic effects in humans.

To aid in the discovery of new environmental risks, a disease detection program should be established, based on continuing surveillance of particular groups of people who are or have been exposed to chemicals known to be animal carcinogens but not yet identified as human carcinogens. Exposure may sometimes be defined by body burden, the level of substances accumulated within the body.

We recommend programs to improve health statistics and facilitate epidemiological studies, so that environmental hazards may be discovered early and dose–response relationships of pollutants better determined. Long-term epidemiological studies are often impeded by difficulties in establishing the fact of death and determining which state has recorded the death certificate. We recommend that a National Death Index be established to provide this information. (We recognize that facilitating access to already available information involves some loss of privacy.) In addition, there should be further study of the comparability and completeness of occupations reported on death certificates and in the census.

Since most pollutants that impair health may first be discovered in the industrial environment, where exposure is intense and relatively uncomplicated by other pollutants, the possibility should be explored of making occupational health statistics more useful for studying the effects of environmental hazards. Employee work records should be retained by employers for a length of time sufficient to permit epidemiological studies. There may be a need to compare different records for the same individual in order to follow and relate occupational, residential, and medical history. An interagency task force should weigh the benefits of this and other comparisons of records against their monetary and social costs, which include possible invasions of privacy.

Surveillance of Animals and Plants Monitoring for surveillance of animals and plants should include productivity, diversity, fecundity, bioaccumulation, and other important aspects of biological species on plots in natural ecosystems; and productivity of major agricultural crops, forage, and forests on selected field plots. In addition, periodic regional surveys should be made of those biological species, including microorganisms, that indicate trends in environmental quality.

● *We recommend that EPA coordinate and support long-term monitoring of certain natural, managed, and damaged ecosystems to identify and assess chronic effects of environmental quality.*

COORDINATION OF MONITORING ACTIVITIES

An Office of Science would facilitate coordination of environmental monitoring activities, especially among EPA and state and local agencies, by working cooperatively with them to improve monitoring. Some of the current fragmentation of monitoring is the result of legislation in which Congress has included excessively detailed specifications for data collection.

● *We recommend that monitoring information and reporting require-ments imposed by legislation and EPA regulations be reviewed and changes suggested in those that decrease the effectiveness of monitoring programs or impose unnecessary costs. EPA should conduct such a review cooperatively with federal, state, and local agencies.* (See Chapter 4.)

Data relevant to environmental management are collected by many federal agencies. Their efforts must be coordinated, particularly so that data on environmental quality can be related to data on health and ecological effects, and so that EPA can monitor the responses of humans, animals, and plants to changes in environmental quality. EPA alone, however, cannot provide this coordination.

● *We recommend that a National Committee on Environmental Monitor-ing be established to coordinate federal environmental monitoring efforts.* (See Chapter 4.)

Executive Summary
of the
Report of the
Committee for Study of
Environmental Manpower

The Executive Summary provides a brief description of the study, along with the Committee's conclusions and recommendations emphasizing the need for a well-coordinated environmental manpower program and for experienced professional competence in the development and administration of the regulations under which EPA must fulfill its responsibilities. The Committee suggests particular attention to conclusions and recommendations numbers 1, 2, 3, and 11.

INTRODUCTION

Manpower aspects of pollution control are a key factor in carrying out the nation's goals for improving environmental conditions. Shortages of well-trained and experienced manpower can slow the development of control technologies, affect program administration, cause inefficient control plant operation and process failures, and boost the costs of achieving environmental controls. Numerous complex and interrelated factors are involved in assuring that the supply of and demand for trained and experienced people are well balanced. The Environmental Protection Agency (EPA) has responsibilities in this regard that are explicitly called for by existing statutes, implicit in the intent of the Congress, and inherent in Agency leadership in these matters, either in meeting defined responsibilities or in seeking clarification of EPA's role.

The national pollution control effort has relied in general on traditional market mechanisms to generate and allocate human resources, but

72

concern exists in this case about the effectiveness of these mechanisms. The Committee concludes that a large-scale or general shortage of pollution control manpower is not now apparent or likely to develop in the near future. Since this conclusion does not call for action, it is not included with the recommendations that follow. It is possible, however, that shortages will occur in selected, specialized occupations. The Committee notes a possible lack of appreciation by EPA of the value of using engineers and scientists who are experienced in pollution abatement. Also, it is apparent that the quality of the current environmental work force could be upgraded through supplemental training and improvements in the educational process.

CONCLUSIONS AND RECOMMENDATIONS

PRIORITY OF MANPOWER POLICIES

Conclusion 1

Legislative authorizations, strategies, and levels of activity vary among the several environmental programs. All the programs are affected by legislatively established time schedules, specifically directed responsibility for manpower development, anticipated funding commitments, and environmental interest and performance in the public and private sectors. Yet the emphasis placed by EPA on manpower development has diminished since the Agency's inception. This practice shows the low priority given the manpower aspects of the pollution control effort. (See Chapter 3 and Appendixes A and C.)

Recommendation 1

● *The Committee recommends that Congress clarify its intent for environmental manpower development and training activities in existing legislation and provide EPA with a clear directive concerning its manpower and training authority.*

● *The importance of manpower needs should be recognized by Congress and the Executive and appropriately reflected in the Agency's budget. Manpower planning and training should be adequately funded, and there should be no diversion of manpower planning funds to other activities.*

● *To define and focus environmental manpower responsibilities in EPA, we recommend that a high-level group be established within its headquarters with representation from the regional offices to insure adequate manpower planning and development. This group should coordinate and supplement the activities of manpower planning and training staffs in the program areas of air, water supply, wastewater, solid wastes, and other program elements.*

MANPOWER PLANNING

Conclusion 2

Leadership for planning and developing a national manpower program for environmental pollution control logically rests with EPA. Congress and the Executive Branch should support this effort. Although the Committee concludes that a large-scale or general shortage of pollution control manpower is not now apparent or likely to develop in the near future, shortages may occur in selected, specialized occupations. Changes affecting manpower development and training needs in the environmental field could come rapidly as a result of the following factors: (1) the diversity of skills required among the professional personnel who plan, design, and manage pollution control programs and also among the subprofessionals, some of whom must be highly trained to operate and maintain the pollution control systems; (2) the immensity of the anticipated program in which expenditures during the next 10 years will be several times those of the U.S. space program; (3) the extremely short time span mandated to accomplish this program; and (4) the shift from ambient quality standards to quantitative emission standards in air pollution control. All these will draw heavily upon the nation's finite resources of money, energy, and manpower.

Success will depend on the uninterrupted availability of specialized, highly trained professional manpower to manage national pollution control programs and to conceive, design, construct, and monitor the complex systems needed to meet mandated standards. Many of these systems do not now exist or are in early stages of development. The efficient operation and maintenance of these sophisticated systems will depend upon the availability of highly trained subprofessional manpower.

The many skills required to carry out the programs and to operate control facilities at their designed capacities require that manpower factors be considered in all phases of program development and operation. The Committee concludes that increases in the manpower supply in some specialized fields may not be sufficiently rapid to meet the need within the mandated time. Shortages of trained manpower could result in inefficient plant operations and could waste capital investment and operating funds far in excess of what is required for adequate manpower development and training. (See Chapters 2 and 7.)

Recommendation 2

● *The Committee recommends that EPA present to the Executive Branch and Congress a comprehensive program of support for the development of professional and subprofessional manpower and operators. (The section in Chapter 3 entitled "Present and Proposed Manpower Activities" contains guidelines as to when training programs would be recommended.) This program should be appropriate to the legislated goals of controlling environmental pollution. Such a program should include a long-term strategy for environmental manpower development based on manpower planning and using the most appropriate educational techniques. The manpower program would be implemented at the federal, state, and local levels under the leadership of EPA.*

● *An environmental manpower impact analysis should be made to assure that the professional and highly trained subprofessional manpower required to implement environmental legislation can become available within the prescribed time. This thorough assessment of manpower requirements should be done when legislation is drafted and hearings are held rather than after enactment of the legislation.*

● *EPA should use these impact analyses as a basis for making recommendations to Congress and the Executive Branch concerning programs required to avoid shortages in the manpower necessary to carry out the proposed legislation.* (See Appendixes B and C.)

TECHNICAL INPUT TO EPA DECISION MAKING

Conclusion 3

Since the statutes and regulations under which EPA must act are complex, they require a high level of experienced technical input in operation to avoid conflicting directives and regulations that lead to unnecessary litigation. In the Committee's view, although EPA has many well-qualified technical personnel, there are too few experienced technical personnel at decision-making levels. Unfortunately, there has been substantial confusion in the development of clear, workable guidelines for problem solution, management of construction grants, issuance of permits, and, particularly, in the conduct of enforcement actions. The situation is more complex because EPA is subject to executive policy, Congressional mandates, and court decisions resulting in instances of conflicting operational directives. (See Chapter 3 and Appendix C.)

Recommendation 3

● *EPA should better use its technical personnel to assure that its directives can be accomplished with existing or soon-to-be-available technology.*

MANPOWER COORDINATION AT THE FEDERAL LEVEL

Conclusion 4

Although EPA has the primary role for environmental manpower development, it has not coordinated its programs with the environmental manpower research and training programs carried on by the Department of Health, Education, and Welfare, the Department of Defense, and other federal agencies.

Recommendation 4

● *The Committee recommends that EPA establish a well-coordinated federal manpower planning and training program for environmental control. Such a responsibility should be mandated by Congressional and Executive action.*

ASSISTANCE FOR STATE AND LOCAL AGENCIES

Conclusion 5

Cooperation is needed among various levels of government and the private sector to assess environmental manpower needs and to plan cost–effective programs to meet them.

Many of the training programs for operators and technicians are at state and local levels. These include local school districts, state vocational education programs, community colleges, and federal programs to reduce unemployment, such as those under the Comprehensive Employment and Training Act. Local manpower planning and training are generally limited to those occupational categories where local resources can meet the demand. While local educational programs produce a substantial number of operators and technicians, the dispersed nature of the system makes national summary data difficult to obtain. (See Chapter 4 and Appendix D.)

Recommendation 5

● *The Committee, recognizing that delivery systems for specialized training are largely in the hands of state and local officials, recommends that EPA pursue a three-part strategy to assist in monitoring and mobilizing these resources for pollution control.*

(1) EPA should provide technical assistance and grants to give state and local agencies the tools needed to plan for manpower demands in environmental protection;

(2) EPA, state, and local environmental officials should work with education administrators concerning special training programs. Careful manpower planning is essential in order to make the most effective use of all available resources; and

(3) EPA should identify the gaps in state and local progams and prepare a national assessment of demand and suppy. Working with the U.S. Department of Labor, Office of Education, industry, and professional assocations, EPA should provide leadership in the development of programs to support state and local manpower activities.

PROJECTION MODELS

Conclusion 6

Demands for environmental manpower are strongly affected by legislative action, the resulting EPA regulations, and the national economy. Thus, demand projections, particularly over long periods of time, are highly conditional by nature. The critical importance of policy and economic assumptions to accurate projections must be kept in mind in assessing the validity of such projections. Still, projection models can identify possible imbalances based on the best available information, particularly for incremental analyses involving program changes.

Projections of environmental manpower supply and demand have been subject to a number of deficiencies which are of particular concern to the Committee. Most of these projections have been aggregated at a national level. This makes their use risky, because the comparison of projected supply and demand ignores distances between geographic sources of supply and points of demand. But distances between jobs and potential workers are important, and they are more important in occupational categories whose job-seeking radius tends to be local than in others with a national job market. This aspect of planning is but one of several important behavioral characteristics that are ignored in current projection models, all of which have potentially important impacts on imbalances between the supply of and demand for environmental manpower in different occupational categories. (See Appendix B.)

Recommendation 6

● *The Committee recommends that EPA increase its use of manpower analysis tools that are available both within and outside the Agency for a better understanding of future manpower requirements. Data sources and projection models from the National Science Foundation, Bureau of the Census, and Bureau of Labor Statistics should be used more extensively.*

● *EPA should also strengthen its support for state and local manpower planning. Support should be encouraged from other governmental agencies interested in local labor market planning in order to develop an adequate data base. Emphasis should be placed on a detailed examination of portions of an overall manpower projection model, concentrating on more local or regional problems or both. Efforts should be made to identify those occupational specialities that are critical to effective pollution control.*

● *The Committee further recommends that EPA itself improve its environmental manpower projection methodologies by relying both on staff expertise and advisory committee evaluations. These projections should be disaggregated to specific job groups in each categorical program and to sufficiently small geographic areas to be of use to state and local environmental manpower planners. Much greater emphasis should be placed on accounting for those behavioral characteristics of the environmental labor force that are likely to have a bearing on imbalances between supply and demand, particularly at state and local levels.*

ADVISORY PANEL

Conclusion 7

EPA terminated its limited use of advisory panels in the fields of manpower planning and training. The Committee concludes that the complete absence of regular input from experts to the development of manpower policy is a deficiency that should be corrected. (See Chapter 3.)

Recommendation 7

● *The Committee recommends that a technical panel be established to advise EPA in manpower planning and education. This panel should include experts from state and local agencies, industry, and the academic community. Specifically, the panel should include engineers, scientists, manpower planning specialists, and managers of environmental control systems.*

CHARGES FOR TRAINING

Conclusion 8

EPA's role in conducting training programs in pollution control for personnel not employed by EPA and the charges to participants in these programs have been controversial. These charges have adversely affected participation in the training programs, particularly by state and local employees. Various actions have discouraged EPA from providing direct, specialized instruction. Nonetheless, a need exists for the training of instructors and a capability for the development of training materials. (See Chapter 3.)

Recommendation 8

● *The Committee recommends that EPA make a major effort to develop local institutional arrangements to meet specialized training requirements. EPA should continue to develop training materials where appropriate, and to train instructors. Involvement in direct training should continue on a limited basis. Since participation is constrained when fees are imposed, the Committee recommends that EPA eliminate fees for these training programs.*

RESEARCH, TRAINING, AND TECHNICAL CENTERS

Conclusion 9

Research is an integral component of professional education, particularly in the complex field of environmental control. Therefore, research policy should explicitly embody training objectives as a major element. Furthermore, investment in research helps to build centers of expertise that provide training for the areas in which they are located. These contributions to overall pollution abatement efforts offer lasting and significant results beyond individual project work. This should be recognized by EPA's Office of Research and Development, and research funding should be planned in coordination with the proposed EPA manpower planning group. (See Chapter 4.)

Recommendation 9

● *The Committee recommends that as a means for expediting technology transfer, personnel associated with technically based environmental systems be provided with opportunities to obtain up-to-date career training by association with research activities. Funds should be allocated to educational institutions for development of environmental research and training centers that can serve as such sources of technical assistance to small businesses and government. This recommendation should be accorded a priority high enough to assure student involvement in ongoing studies of pollution abatement and control methodology. Funding for such centers should be awarded on a competitive basis.* (See Chapter 6.)

ENVIRONMENTAL MANPOWER REQUIREMENTS IN THE PRIVATE SECTOR

Conclusion 10

The private sector is a major employer of environmental manpower. Estimates of these manpower requirements can be related to planned environmental expenditures to estimate the magnitude of future needs. Traditionally, larger industries have used in-house and on-the-job training to develop manpower to solve environmental problems and have relied on educational institutions to provide basic education. Although this trend will continue, the emphasis on highly specialized manpower will stimulate additional needs for formal training and continuing education in environmentally related disciplines. Various small business-es, on the other hand, may find themselves confronted by highly technical problems but with no reliable access to needed technical advice on problem-solving capabilities. Therefore, additional assistance must be provided to these firms as well as to individuals. (See Appendix E.)

Recommendation 10

● *(1) EPA should analyze manpower needs for industry and the private sector as these needs are influenced by existing and proposed environmental legislation.*

● *(2) EPA should obtain the participation of private industry in its training mission for environmental manpower. More specifically, student cooperative programs should be extended to potential employees, and continuing education efforts should be enhanced. Private industry should be encouraged to take a more active role in advising the appropriate educational institutions, environmental agencies, and EPA in their assessments of training requirements.*

● *(3) EPA should cooperate closely with the private sector to design and conduct a long-term personnel study to produce the data necessary to assess current personnel use and to project future manpower requirements and training needs.*

● *(4) Congress should appropriate funds to enable local agencies and organizations to provide technical assistance and accurate information to farmers and small businesses unable to afford technical manpower to carry out the objectives of environmental legislation.*

CONTINUITY IN OPERATION OF POLLUTION CONTROL SYSTEMS

Conclusion 11

Most environmental control systems are based upon biological processes that degrade wastes. These systems must be operated on a continuous basis to be effective. If they are not and if the operating environment is not properly controlled, microorganisms die and render the processes inoperative for extended periods of time. One of the most serious obstacles to the continued operation of pollution control systems is work stoppages of environmental control facilities. Interruption of biologically based environmental protection systems can be disastrous, causing damage to the systems, degradation of the environment, and potential impairment of the health of the people. (See Appendix D.)

Recommendation 11

● *EPA should recognize and study the critical necessity for continuous operation of biologically based environmental protection systems and make appropriate recommendations to Congress concerning solutions to this problem.*

III

COLLATING INDEX
TO THE
COMMITTEE REPORTS

The purpose of this "collating" index is to enable the reader to collect, compare, and integrate certain topics that recur frequently throughout the NRC analytical studies. It is not comprehensive or exhaustive in its inclusion of topics, like more conventional indexes. Instead, it is designed for the analytical reader to approach in two complementary ways: it is short enough to be used as a guide to all the reports, leading the reader to discussions of particular interest; and it can serve to document the existence of themes or coinciding observations in the separate studies that support or contribute perspectives on certain general conclusions and recommendations.

The version of the index included here, however, is a working draft. The reader is referred only to volumes (the Roman numerals) and chapters (the Arabic numerals): page references at this stage of shifting manuscript preparation would have been meaningless. The reader will also notice that not every volume in the series of analytical studies (see Table 2 in this report) has been referenced here. Where this is so, the particular report had either not yet been completed or was still undergoing such extensive revision as this volume went to the printer that its inclusion here was not practicable.

The index itself will, therefore, undergo further revision between now and completion of the entire program. Current plans call for a final version to be printed under separate cover by fall 1977. It will carry page references to the published studies and will be available, to readers who request it, from the Commission on Natural Resources.

L

Laboratory certification, nongovernment, II, 3
Land use, VI, 2
Legislation—decision-making effects, II, 2, 3, 6; III, 1, 5; VI, 1; VII, 3
Legislation—research justification interaction, III, 1

M

Man–environment interaction, II, 2, 3; III, 1
Management objectives
  alternatives, X, 4
  cost–effectiveness studies, VI, 4
  effluent charges and standards, II, 6
  field–staff relationships, II, 2; XI
  incentives, VI, 4
  legislative requirements, X, 4
  materials disposal, X, 4
  modeling, X, 4, 5
  planning and management systems effectiveness, XI
  pollution abatement, X, 4
  prediction analysis, X, 5
  proposal reviews, III, 4
  residuals, VI, 2
  risks, VI, 4
  site selection, X, 5
  strategies characteristics, II, 3, 6; VI, 4; X, 4
  structure, III, 4; XI
Manpower
  analytical requirements studies, V, App. C.
  assessment statistics, V, App. B
  behavioral characteristics, V, App. B
  certification, V, App. E
  Committee for Study of Environmental Manpower, I, 2; V
  certification, V, App. E
  data analysis, V, App. B
  development, V, 1, 3, 7, App. B
  expenditures, pollution control facilities construction, V, App. E

facilities and location, III, 4
federal employment, V, App. C
forecasting, V, App. B
geographical distribution, V, App. B
government employment, V, App. B
incentives, III, 4
industry employment, V, App. B, E
interagency research and development, V, App. B
labor market studies, V, 2
national environmental research strategy, III, 1
national survey, V, App. B
needs, I, 2; II, 2; III, 4; V, 1, 2, 4, 7; App. B, C, E
occupation development, V, 2
occupational distribution, V, App. C
peer review, II, 2, 3, 5; III, 4
planning statutes, V, 1, 2, 3
pollution control labor costs, V, App. E
projections, V, 5, 6, App. B
promotional opportunities, III, 4
quality, V, 7
requirements, legislative objectives, V, App. C
research and development employment, V, App. B
scientific research personnel, III, 4
small business, V, App. E
strategy needs, V, 3
studies, I, 2; V, App. B, E
supply and demand, III, 4; V, App. B
Manpower development
  Congressional definition, V, 1, 7
  directives, V, 3
  forecasting, V, App. B
  management needs, V, 3
Marine Protection Research and Sanctuaries Act, 1972, X, 1, 4
Marine environment (*see* terms beginning with Ocean)
Maumee River, monitoring programs, IV, 3

APPENDIX:
ROSTERS OF
COMMITTEE
MEMBERSHIP

STEERING COMMITTEE FOR ANALYTICAL STUDIES
FOR THE U.S. ENVIRONMENTAL PROTECTION AGENCY

(See the front matter.)

COMMITTEE ON ENVIRONMENTAL DECISION MAKING
(CEDM)

Jack P. Ruina *(Chairman)*, Massachusetts Institute of Technology
Spurgeon M. Keeny *(Vice-Chairman)*, The MITRE Corporation,
McLean, Virginia

PANEL ON SCIENTIFIC AND TECHNICAL CONSIDERATIONS (CEDM)

James A. Fay *(Chairman)*, Massachusetts Institute of Technology
Mario C. Battigelli, University of North Carolina
James N. Butler, Harvard University
Marvin L. Goldberger, Princeton University
John R. Goldsmith, California State Department of Public Health
Milton Harris, Consultant, Washington, D.C.
Daniel A. Okun, University of North Carolina
Fred H. Tschirley, Michigan State University

PANEL ON ORGANIZATIONAL AND SOCIAL CONSIDERATIONS (CEDM)

Philip L. Johnson *(Chairman)*, Oak Ridge Associated Universities
Samuel G. Booras, Institute for Environmental Quality, State of Illinois
Richard M. Cyert, Carnegie-Mellon University
J. Clarence Davies, Conservation Foundation, Washington, D.C.
John D. Steinbruner, Yale University

PANEL ON LEGAL CONSIDERATIONS (CEDM)

Richard B. Stewart *(Chairman)*, Harvard University
Harold P. Green, George Washington University
N. William Hines, University of Iowa
Helen M. Ingram, University of Arizona
Albert J. Rosenthal, Columbia University

PANEL ON EVALUATIVE AND INTEGRATING PROCEDURES (CEDM)

Charles J. Hitch *(Chairman)*, Resources for the Future, Washington, D.C.

99

Robert Dorfman, Harvard University
Howard R. Raiffa, Harvard University
William Schwartz, Tufts University
Myron Tribus, Massachusetts Institute of Technology

ENVIRONMENTAL RESEARCH ASSESSMENT COMMITTEE (ERAC)

John M. Neuhold *(Chairman)*, Utah State University
Bernard B. Berger *(Vice-Chairman)*, University of Massachusetts, Amherst
Timothy Atkeson, Steptoe and Johnson, Washington, D.C.
Norman H. Brooks, California Institute of Technology
A.W. Castleman, Jr., University of Colorado
George M. Hidy, Environmental Research and Technology, Westlake Village, California
William B. House, Midwest Research Institute, Kansas City, Missouri
Paul Kotin, Johns-Manville Corporation, Denver
John P. Mahlstede, Iowa State University
Duncan T. Patten, Arizona State University
Clifford S. Russell, Resources for the Future, Washington, D.C.
Richard J. Sullivan, Stevens Institute of Technology

PANEL ON SOURCES AND CONTROL TECHNIQUES (ERAC)

Bernard B. Berger *(Chairman)*, University of Massachusetts, Amherst
Frederick R. Anderson, Jr., Environmental Law Institute, Washington, D.C.
Blair T. Bower, Consultant, Arlington, Virginia
Robert J. Budnitz, Lawrence Berkeley Laboratory, California
W. Wesley Eckenfelder, Jr., Vanderbilt University
Melvin W. First, Harvard University
Bernd Kahn, Georgia Institute of Technology
Raymond C. Loehr, Cornell University
Clifford S. Russell, Resources for the Future, Washington, D.C.
Melvin W. Webber, University of California, Berkeley

PANEL ON FATES OF POLLUTANTS (ERAC)

A.W. Castleman, Jr. *(Chairman)*, University of Colorado
George M. Hidy *(Vice-Chairman)*, Environmental Research and Technology, Inc., Westlake Village, California

Charles F. Eno, University of Florida
E. Paul Lichtenstein, University of Wisconsin
Theodore G. Metcalf, University of New Hampshire
James J. Morgan, California Institute of Technology
Donald J. O'Connor, Manhattan College
Robert V. O'Neill, Oak Ridge National Laboratory
John M. Wood, University of Minnesota

PANEL ON EFFECTS OF AMBIENT ENVIRONMENTAL QUALITY (ERAC)

Paul Kotin *(Chairman)*, Johns-Manville Corporation, Denver
Jay S. Jacobson *(Vice-Chairman)*, Boyce Thompson Institute, Yonkers, New York
Timothy Atkeson, Steptoe and Johnson, Washington, D.C.
William E. Cooper, Michigan State University
A. Myrick Freeman, III, Bowdoin College
William B. House, Midwest Research Institute, Kansas City, Missouri
George D. Robinson, Center for Environment and Man, Hartford, Connecticut
Joan M. Spyker, University of Arkansas
Lucille F. Stickel, Patuxent Wildlife Research Center, Laurel, Maryland
H. Eldon Sutton, The University of Texas at Austin
Carl J. Wessel, Tracor Jitco, Inc., Rockville, Maryland
Warren Winkelstein, Jr., University of California, Berkeley

PANEL ON ENVIRONMENTAL IMPACTS OF RESOURCES MANAGEMENT (ERAC)

Duncan T. Patten *(Chairman)*, Arizona State University
Suzanne E. Bayley, University of Florida
Perry J. Brown, Colorado State University
Leo Eisel, Illinois Department of Transporation
Charles Fairhurst, University of Minnesota
Charles A.S. Hall, Cornell University
Joseph C. Headley, University of Missouri, Columbia
Cyrus M. McKell, Utah State University
Giulio Pontecorvo, Columbia University
Henry J. Vaux, University of California, Berkeley
Julian Wolpert, Princeton University

STUDY GROUP ON ENVIRONMENTAL MONITORING (SGEM)

John W. Pratt *(Chairman)*, Harvard University
Walter Langbein *(Vice-Chairman)*, U.S. Geological Survey, Reston, Virginia
R. Stephen Berry, University of Chicago
Ralph C. d'Arge, University of Wyoming
Morris DeGroot, Carnegie-Mellon University
Virgil Freed, Oregon State University
John Kinosian, California State Air Resources Board
Marvin Kuschner, State University of New York at Stony Brook
Walter A. Lyon, Pennsylvania Department of Environmental Resources
Brian MacMahon, Harvard University
David E. Reichle, Oak Ridge National Laboratory

PANEL ON AMBIENT MONITORING (SGEM)

Morris DeGroot *(Chairman)*, Carnegie-Mellon University
Myron B. Fiering, Harvard University
Walter I. Goldburg, University of Pittsburgh
Glenn R. Hilst, The Research Corporation, Wethersfield, Connecticut
John Kinosian, California State Air Resources Board
Walter Langbein, U.S. Geological Survey, Reston, Virginia
Mervin E. Muller, The World Bank, Washington, D.C.

PANEL ON SOURCE MONITORING (SGEM)

Walter A. Lyon *(Chairman)*, Pennsylvania Department of Environmental Resources
Francis J. Anscombe, Yale University
R. Stephen Berry, University of Chicago
Paul M. Berthouex, University of Wisconsin
Virgil Freed, Oregon State University
Richard W. Gerstle, PEDCo-Environmental, Cincinnati, Ohio

PANEL ON EFFECTS MONITORING (SGEM)

Marvin Kuschner *(Chairman)*, State University of New York at Stony Brook
Rita R. Colwell, University of Maryland
Ralph d'Arge, University of Wyoming

Leonard Hamilton, Brookhaven National Laboratory
Herbert C. Jones III, Tennessee Valley Authority, Muscle Shoals, Alabama
Dean Krueger, George Washington University
James V. Neel, University of Michigan
David Reichle, Oak Ridge National Laboratory

COMMITTEE FOR STUDY OF ENVIRONMENTAL MANPOWER (CSEM)

Earnest F. Gloyna *(Chairman)*, The University of Texas at Austin
Robert McGinnis *(Vice-Chairman)*, Cornell University
Lilia Abron-Robinson, Howard University
Patrick R. Atkins, Aluminum Company of America, Pittsburgh
Michael S. Baram, Massachusetts Institute of Technology
John Cairns, Jr., Virginia Polytechnic Institute and State University
C.W. Cook, General Foods Corporation, White Plains, New York
Hugh H. Folk, University of Illinois
John H. Ludwig, Consultant, Santa Barbara, California
Monroe T. Morgan, East Tennessee State University
John D. Parkhurst, Los Angeles County Sanitation Districts, Whittier
Ernest T. Smerdon, The University of Texas System, Austin
Gerald W. Thomas, New Mexico State University

PANEL ON METHODOLOGY AND NATIONAL DATA ASPECTS (CSEM)

Robert McGinnis *(Chairman)*, Cornell University
Hugh H. Folk *(Vice-Chairman)*, University of Illinois
Lilia Abron-Robinson, Howard University
David W. Breneman, Brookings Institution, Washington, D.C.
Robert A. Canham, Water Pollution Control Federation, Washington, D.C.
Neal H. Rosenthal, Bureau of Labor Statistics, Washington, D.C.

PANEL ON LEGAL ASPECTS (CSEM)

Michael S. Baram *(Chairman)*, Massachusetts Institute of Technology
Thomas B. Bracken, Bracken, Selig and Padnos, Boston
Corwin W. Johnson, The University of Texas at Austin
David H. Marks, Massachusetts Institute of Technology

PANEL ON FEDERAL ASPECTS (CSEM)

Ernest T. Smerdon *(Chairman)*, The University of Texas System, Austin
John Cairns, Jr., Virginia Polytechnic Institute and State University
Wallace L. Gatewood, Florida State University
Joseph McCabe, American Society of Civil Engineers, New York
Gordon E. McCallum, Engineering Science, Inc., Washington, D.C.
Monroe T. Morgan, East Tennessee State University

PANEL ON STATE AND LOCAL ASPECTS (CSEM)

John D. Parkhurst *(Chairman)*, Los Angeles County Sanitation Districts, Whittier
Robert V. Daigh, California State Water Resources Control Board, Sacramento
Herbert W. Grubb, Texas Water Development Board, Austin
John H. Ludwig, Consultant, Santa Barbara, California
Nicholas Pohlit, National Environmental Health Association, Denver

PANEL ON INDUSTRY AND PRIVATE SECTOR ASPECTS (CSEM)

Patrick R. Atkins *(Chairman)*, Aluminum Company of America, Pittsburgh
John D. Alden, Engineering Manpower Commission, New York
C.W. Cook, General Foods Corporation, White Plains, New York
Walter A. Hamilton, The Conference Board, New York
James R. Mahoney, Environmental Research and Technology, Inc., Concord, Massachusetts
Gerald W. Thomas, New Mexico State University

COMMITTEE ON ENERGY AND THE ENVIRONMENT (CEE)

Stanley I. Auerbach *(Chairman)*, Oak Ridge National Laboratory
Frank L. Parker *(Vice-Chairman)*, Vanderbilt University
Davis B. Bobrow, University of Maryland
Robert Dorfman, Harvard University
Joseph Feinstein, Varian Associates, Palo Alto
James R. Jones, Peabody Coal Company, St. Louis
James E. Krier, University of California, Los Angeles
Daniel P. Loucks, Cornell University
Marc J. Roberts, Harvard University
Liane B. Russell, Oak Ridge National Laboratory

Carl M. Shy, University of North Carolina
James E. Watson, Tennessee Valley Authority, Chattanooga

PANEL ON ELECTRIC POWER (CEE)

Frank L. Parker *(Chairman)*, Vanderbilt University
James L. Cooley, University of Georgia
James R. Jones, Peabody Coal Company, St. Louis
Marc J. Roberts, Harvard University
Liane B. Russell, Oak Ridge National Laboratory
William B. Russell, Oak Ridge National Laboratory
James Sawyer, Resources for the Future, Inc., Washington, D.C.
Carl M. Shy, University of North Carolina
Arnold J. Silverman, University of Montana
James E. Watson, Tennessee Valley Authority

PANEL ON AUTOMOTIVE INTERACTIONS (CEE)

Joseph Feinstein *(Chairman)*, Varian Associates, Palo Alto
Henry Warren Art, Williams College
Davis B. Bobrow, University of Maryland
Bruce Goeller, RAND Corporation, Santa Monica
James E. Krier, University of California, Los Angeles
Daniel P. Loucks, Cornell University
Vaun A. Newill, Exxon Research and Engineering Company, Linden, New Jersey
Sam Peltzman, University of Chicago
Richard Stewart, Harvard University
William L. Templeton, Battelle, Pacific Northwest Laboratories

OTHER PARTICIPANTS (CEE)

H.L. Balzan, Tennessee Valley Authority, Chattanooga
Clayton D. McAuliff, Chevron Oil Field Research Company, La Habra, California
Virginia Nolan, University of San Diego

COMMITTEE ON MULTIMEDIUM APPROACH TO SLUDGE MANAGEMENT

Harvey O. Banks *(Chairman)*, Consultant, Belmont, California
Vinton W. Bacon, University of Wisconsin, Milwaukee

Richard I. Dick, University of Delaware
Richard B. Engdahl, Battelle Columbus Laboratories
Arden R. Gaufin, University of Utah
M. Grant Gross, The Johns Hopkins University
Orie L. Loucks, University of Wisconsin, Madison
Mitchell Wendell, Consultant, McLean, Virginia
Jean O. Williams, Office of the Governor of Texas

COMMITTEE ON PESTICIDE REGULATION

William G. Eden *(Chairman)*, Lawson State College
Perry L. Adkisson, Texas A&M University
Morris F. Cranmer, National Center for Toxicological Research, Jefferson, Arkansas
John E. Davies, University of Miami Medical School
Vincent Giglio, Florida Department of Agriculture and Consumer Service
Edward H. Glass, New York State Agriculture Experiment Station, Geneva
Robert E. Hamman, CIBA-GEIGY Corporation, Greensboro, North Carolina
Joseph C. Headley, University of Missouri, Columbia
Joseph J. Hickey, University of Wisconsin, Madison
Charles E. Palm, Cornell University
Tony J. Peterle, Ohio State University
Keith R. Shea, U.S. Department of Agriculture, Washington, D.C.
Philip J. Spear, National Pest Control Association, Inc., Vienna, Virginia
Lucille F. Stickel, Patuxent Wildlife Research Center, Laurel, Maryland
Dan A. Tarlock, Indiana University
Gerald T. Weekman, North Carolina State University

PANEL ON THE ACQUISITION AND USE
OF DATA AT THE FEDERAL AND STATE LEVELS

Federal Subpanel

Robert E. Hamman, CIBA-GEIGY Corporation, Greensboro, North Carolina
Morris F. Cranmer, National Center for Toxicological Research, Jefferson, Arkansas
Charles E. Palm, Cornell University
Tony J. Peterle, Ohio State University

Keith R. Shea, U.S. Department of Agriculture, Washington, D.C.
Philip J. Spear, National Pest Control Association, Vienna, Virginia
Dan A. Tarlock, Indiana University

State Subpanel

Vincent Giglio, Florida Department of Agriculture and Consumer
Services
Joseph J. Hickey, University of Wisconsin, Madison
Gerald T. Weekman, North Carolina State University

PANEL ON IMPACTS OF EPA PESTICIDE REGULATIONS
IN THE UNITED STATES

Edward H. Glass, New York State Agricultural Experiment Station,
Geneva
Dan A. Tarlock, Indiana University
Lucille F. Stickel, Patuxent Wildlife Research Center, Laurel, Maryland

PANEL ON PESTICIDE REGULATORY
DECISIONS IN OTHER COUNTRIES

John E. Davies *(Chairman)*, University of Miami Medical School
Perry L. Adkisson, Texas A&M University
William G. Eden, Pell City, Alabama
Edward H. Glass, New York State Agricultural Experiment Station,
Geneva
Joseph C. Headly, University of Missouri, Columbia
Keith R. Shea, U.S. Department of Agriculture, Washington, D.C.
Gerald T. Weekman, North Carolina State University

COMMITTEE ON SOCIETAL CONSEQUENCES OF TRANSPORTATION NOISE ABATEMENT

William Baumol *(Chairman)*, Princeton University, New York University
Elizabeth D. Bennett, Massachusetts Institute of Technology
D.E. Broadbent, Oxford University
Arthur DeVany, Texas A&M University
Kenneth Eldred, Bolt Beranek & Newman, Inc., Cambridge, Massachu-
setts
Alan Freeman, University of Minnesota
Marcia Gelpe, University of Minnesota

David Glass, Russell Sage Foundation, New York
David M. Green, Harvard University
Calvin S. Hamilton, Director of Planning, City of Los Angeles
Edward K. Morlok, University of Pennsylvania
Jon Nelson, Pennsylvania State University
William Sampson, Northwestern University
A.A. Walters, World Bank, Washington, D.C.

OCEAN DISPOSAL STUDY STEERING COMMITTEE

Donn S. Gorsline *(Chairman)*, University of Southern California
Robert C. Beardsley, Massachusetts Institute of Technology
Duncan C. Blanchard, State University of New York, Albany
Edward D. Goldberg, University of California
Roy W. Hann, Jr., Texas A&M University
John J. Lee, City College of New York
William G. Pearcy, Oregon State University
Francis A. Richards, University of Washington
Larry S. Slotta, Oregon State University

REVIEW COMMITTEE ON THE
MANAGEMENT OF EPA'S
RESEARCH AND DEVELOPMENT ACTIVITIES

Robert W. Berliner *(Chairman)*, Yale University School of Medicine
Ivan L. Bennett, New York University Medical Center
Hendrick W. Bode, Harvard University
Ralph E. Gomory, International Business Machines Corporation
Milton Harris, Consultant, Washington, D.C.
John M. Neuhold, Utah State University